Pop It, S

Fix It, Serve It

Also by Laura Karr

The Can Opener Gourmet

Pop It, Stir It, Fix It, Serve It

CAN-DO COOKING

Laura Karr

HYPERION New York

Library of Congress Cataloging-in-Publication Data

Karr, Laura
    Pop it, stir it, fix it, serve it: can-do cooking / Laura Karr.— 1st ed.
      p.   cm.
    ISBN 0-7868-8860-1
    1. Cookery (Canned foods)   2. Quick and easy cookery.   I. Title.

TX821.K27   2005
641.5'55—dc22

                                                          2004042431

Hyperion books are available for special promotions and premiums. For details
    contact Michael Rentas, Assistant Director, Inventory Operations, Hyperion,
77 West 66th Street, 11th floor, New York, New York 10023, or call 212-456-0133.

FIRST EDITION

10 9 8 7 6 5 4 3 2 1

For Chris Agnew

Contents

Acknowledgments

Luckily, by the time you mail off a cookbook manuscript to the publisher, you've forgetten just how much work it was to write. But at this moment, I'm still in awe of my grandma, Laura Elizabeth Karr, and my father, James Karr, who not only kept up with me through this entire process, but said, "Thank you, Sir, may I have another!"

As my deadline loomed closer, just knowing they were there to do recipe testing and backup testing became a huge comfort to me, since it was one enormous detail that I didn't have to worry about. I know I couldn't have finished on time without their dedication and encouragement.

I have to thank my agent, Liv Blumer, also. She's the voice of calm and has a way of making you feel that you're perfectly normal for loving your book but wanting it out of your life forever (or at least sent away to camp for the summer).

I also want to thank Will Schwalbe, editor-in-chief at Hyperion, for seeing this project through when it was an editorless orphan.

There were many other people who helped kitchen-test these recipes. My cousins Julie and Kevin Reager, and Michele and Brad Reager, helped a great deal. I'd also like to thank Lori Aretz, Heather Ash and Dominic Cianciolo, Sally Bisher, Cheryl and Todd Caine, Todd Gearou, Penny Karr, Don and Tona Killingworth, Justin McFarr and Lynn Marcinko, Scott and Sheila Petri, Glenda Reager, Kelly and Michelle Reager, Bud and Geri Reager, John Redmon, Vicki Sapunor, Carol and Harvey Snyder, Preston Wertheimer, and Sabine Whipple.

In addition, I'd like to thank Ann Wexler for her unwavering support and encouragement over the years. I also want to thank David Orr and Adam Biddle for superb video production services. Thanks to Marsha Vernoga for being a reference dietician as well as a kitchen tester. Thanks to Neil Patel, Creative and Relentless Marketing Guy Extraordinaire. Thanks to Wayne Williams (and his lovely wife, Marsha) for cover photography that was painless. Thanks also go to my tag team of editors: Natalie Kaire, Ben Loehnen, and Kiera Hepford.

And finally, I'd like to thank Chris Agnew for his constant support, for being someone I can truly count on, and for being someone who makes me believe it's all going to be okay.

Pop It, Stir It, Fix It, Serve It

Introduction

Several years ago I needed to supplement my diet with vitamins and minerals. The catch was, I found that all those pills tasted terrible and were difficult to swallow. I actually caught myself thinking, "Man, they can put phones in our cars, so why can't they make chewable vitamins and minerals that taste good?" And then I remembered that they did—it was called "food."

Frankly, it's a little embarrassing to admit that. I suppose I just felt too busy to eat right all the time, and then when I didn't, it was easy to just give up, as if not eating right once made the whole house of cards collapse.

But after the food-vitamin "revelation," I promised myself I would do better. Instead of taking nutritional shortcuts by swallowing a bunch of pills, I would really make the effort to eat nutritious food that contained adequate amounts of vitamins and minerals. I was simply going to have to take my shortcuts elsewhere.

In my first book, *The Can Opener Gourmet*™, I told the story of how I came up with the idea for a cookbook that uses canned foods. The above-mentioned nutritional aspect is another piece of that story.

And after researching those foods I "never" used (no one seems to count olives, corn, soup, or tomato sauce as "canned" food), I decided that they were not only okay to use as shortcuts, they were a valuable source of ready nutrition. I also decided that I didn't have to use them in the way that my mother and her mother did (i.e., casseroles containing canned soup); I could make new combinations using foods we eat more of today.

Since the *Can Opener Gourmet*™ was published, there has been a much broader acceptance of kitchen shortcuts that use prepackaged goods. And while I think that's okay sometimes, I'm still committed to canned and jarred foods because they are generally free of chemical preservatives.

I've also heard from readers since then who came up with uses for *The Can Opener Gourmet*™ that I hadn't thought of, some very gratifying. One woman wrote to say that since she had become disabled she couldn't cook, but with this book, she could. Another told me she tucked the book into all the food baskets her company donated during the holidays. Another mentioned the hurricane weather and snow they had on the East Coast, something I hadn't had to worry about here in California. And now that baby boomers are hitting the road in RVs in record numbers, it comes in useful there, too.

So getting back to this book, in the first chapter I'll review a little about canned foods, their benefits, what more I've learned about them, and nutrition. If you read the first book and feel comfortable with cans, just plunge into this new batch of recipes. If this is your first foray into the canned-food world, you'll probably be shocked at how long canned foods have been around and how nutritionally sound and pure they are.

There's one last thing I feel the need to mention, as I did in the first book. I've developed these recipes in their simplest format, which means I've used dried spices. I also give equivalents and rules of thumb for fresh spices if you have them on hand or prefer to use them. But if you're a little leery about using dried spices, remember that many Indian dishes rely heavily on them, and those are some amazing dishes. So, *bon appétit!*

What's So Grand About Canned?

CHAPTER 1

THEY'RE NATURAL FOODS, YET PEST-FREE

* Canned food is nearly always *preservative-free*. That's because the heat process sterilizes the food and the vacuum process preserves it indefinitely, making preservatives unnecessary.

* Commercial canning *eliminates as much as 99 percent of the pesticide residues* occasionally found in fresh produce.

* Canning also *destroys bacteria* that cause food spoilage. This is accomplished through the normal washing, peeling, blanching, and heat processing of canned fruits and vegetables.

* Canned tuna *does not carry the risk of histamine poisoning,* as does fresh tuna.

* Baby food, which is used in some of my recipes, is one of the purest foods available—usually consisting of just the fruit or vegetable pureed with a little water.

THEY SEAL IN NUTRITION, AND LOTS OF IT

* Because fruits and vegetables are generally harvested at their peak and then quickly heat-sterilized and sealed, canned items *do not lose their nutritional potency* in the same way as many "fresh" foods that sit in warehouses, then in trucks, and then on grocery shelves.

* Canned foods are *preserved in their own juices,* which contain much nutritional value that is often lost with many home-cooking methods.

A BRIEF HISTORY

As Napoleon once said, "An army marches on its stomach." Trouble was, pillaging and plundering makes an army hungry, and food only lasted so long and for so many miles back then. So in 1795, Napoleon offered a reward of 12,000 francs to anyone who could find a way to preserve food.

It took fourteen years, but in 1809 Nicolas Appert collected the reward for his method of putting food inside a jar or bottle, heating it, and sealing it until needed. (I always wonder how many cases of food poisoning he got and if, in retrospect, he felt the reward was worth it.) It would be another fifty years before Mr. Pasteur unraveled the mystery of how heat killed microorganisms responsible for food spoilage.

Not to be outdone, a year later the English developed tin-coated iron cans to replace the glass (pillaging and plundering is also hard on breakables). This technology spread to America a few years later, and by the end of the nineteenth century, the first automatic can-making machines were introduced.

But food preservation and storage aren't the only advantages cans have going for them—they also offer some surprising health and convenience benefits.

* Professional food processors have *already calculated nutritional values* for you in accordance with government requirements, making it easier for you to make health-conscious decisions.

* Although the body needs some salt to function normally, *many canned foods offer no- or low-sodium alternatives* for those wishing to curb salt intake.

* Rinsing canned foods in a colander under cold water can *reduce sodium content up to 40 percent*.

* Tomatoes contain important antioxidants such as lycopene. Lycopene is a pigment that gives fruits and vegetables their red color, and has been credited with helping to prevent cancer and other diseases. The American Dietetic Association (ADA) cites research that says more lycopene is absorbed from cooked tomatoes than from raw. As a result, canned tomato products (like diced tomatoes, tomato sauce, or tomato puree) are among the best sources of dietary lycopene.

* *Canned tuna, salmon, and sardines contain omega-3 fatty acids,* which are thought to help protect against heart disease.

* Canned beans *retain their high fiber content* through the canning process.

* The ADA also reports that *canned fish contain more calcium than the same amount of freshly cooked* fish.

THEY'RE GOOD FOR YOUR BUSY LIFE

Canned food:

* keeps virtually forever.

* is readily available year-round, in season or not.

* is already prepared for use—chopped, diced, pureed, etc.—allowing you to exchange kitchen time for more free time.

* helps turn time in the kitchen into time with the family because it's so easy to use, even children can help—just assemble, season, and heat.

THEY'RE VERSATILE, FITTING MANY LIFESTYLES AND CULTURES

Canned food:

* offers great variety—1,500 types of foods are available.

* fits many nutritional and culinary trends.

* is an easy way to bring new flavors and foods from different cultures to your table.

* is environmentally friendly—more than 90 percent of canned items are packaged in recyclable steel, with approximately 20,000 steel cans being recycled in the United States every minute.

A FEW TIPS

After you read this section or before you go grocery shopping, you may want to see Appendix 2, "Stocking Your Pantry," beginning on page 319. You may use it as a straight shopping list to thoroughly supply your cupboards or as a decision-making guide in your pantry, taking into consideration your cooking and storage requirements.

Bargains
I have great luck at those "everything's a dollar" type stores. I get crab and shrimp for a dollar per 6-ounce can. I also find two or three cans of vegetables for 99¢. I've found that certain closeout stores carry everything from clothing to furniture to canned goods. Sometimes you can get great prices at large drugstores. Just keep a look out.

Dietary Concerns
Canned food is known for being high in salt, but that's not always the case. For instance, most people are shocked to find that tomato puree averages only 15 milligrams of sodium per ¼-cup serving. If you need to watch your sodium intake, become an avid label reader, and remember the rinsing-under-cold-water trick. (Please note that rinsing may also wash away some nutrients.) But there are also low-salt, low-fat, and low-sugar versions of many canned foods. Just keep in mind that you may need to increase some other flavors to compensate.

Expiration Dates
Expiration dates are rarely found on canned foods since they last virtually forever if stored properly. In fact, biologically sound canned food has been found in ships that sank more than one hundred years ago. Taste may fade a bit over that kind of time, however.

But you may have noticed numbers imprinted on the bottom of some cans. Those are manufacturers' internal codes, which tell them when and where the foods were processed.

In addition, some companies are now including a "freshness/use by" date with their products.

However, the general rule of thumb is this: Canned goods will remain fresh in your pantry for two years after the date of purchase. They actually have an indefinite shelf life if stored at 75°F or less. And whether the flavor may have faded a little or not, the foods still retain all their nutritional value and are perfectly safe to eat well after two years.

Safety

Some cans hiss slightly when opened, which is a normal result of vacuum packing. But if a can practically explodes or spurts when opened, it's possible that the food could be spoiled. Likewise, if the can is severely dented or bulging, don't buy it. When in doubt, throw it out or return it to your grocery store. Slight dents are not a problem, though. Just use your best judgment.

In addition, I've also learned that canned foods are one of the safest ways for people with low white blood cell counts (such as transplant or chemotherapy patients) to get fruits and vegetables. Again, that's because the washing, heat sterilizing, and vacuum packing get rid of bacteria and up to 99 percent of pesticide residue. Raw fruits and vegetables, dried fruits, and frozen foods may have harmful contaminants.

Storing Leftovers

If you don't use the entire contents of a can, you may cover it and refrigerate the unused portion, although it is strongly recommended that you transfer the food to a storage container first to avoid the risk of off-flavoring. There's one exception: *Always* transfer tomato products to other (nonmetallic) containers so that the acids don't react with the metal.

Tomatoes

Use canned tomatoes within about six months for best results. While they will keep indefinitely, they can develop a tinny taste over time. Also, because of the strong acid content in tomatoes (as well as lemons and vinegar), stay away from all-aluminum and pure copper pans. They react strongly with the acid and produce a bitter aftertaste. And in the case of copper, the combination can be toxic. Use nonreactive, coated, combination, or stainless-steel pans to be safe.

Evaporated Milk

Most people have seen cans of evaporated milk, yet they have no idea what it is or how it's used. Evaporated milk is simply milk that's twice as concentrated as whole milk because the moisture content has been reduced by 50 to 60 percent.

I use it quite often for sauces, soups, and desserts. It's also a great substitute for half-and-half or even heavy cream. It has less fat than cream, but if you use a thickening agent such as cornstarch, you can easily substitute it in many recipes.

If you want to use milk that's not concentrated, just add an equal amount of water to the evaporated milk. It's quite a lifesaver if you run out of milk for your cereal.

One other thing: I've seen countless cookbooks promising that if you chill evaporated milk and beat it furiously, you can make whipped cream. I have still never succeeded in doing that.

Eggs, Cheese, Butter, and Milk

Each of these foods can be frozen if you follow certain guidelines. Freezing not only provides you with these perishable foods for much longer periods, it also allows you to take advantage of bulk and sale prices. *The Joy of Cooking* provides excellent information with specific instructions on how to package just about anything for freezing, along with guidelines for how long the items may be kept. I've also seen Websites full of such information.

Eggs cannot be frozen in their shells, however. You may freeze whites and yolks separately or together, starting them out in ice trays, for example, then moving them into sealed containers. Just be sure you keep track of how many eggs you put in each parcel for measuring purposes later.

Cheese is another great perishable you can freeze as long as it's grated or shredded first. If you freeze a block, it will be crumbly when it thaws. I find that one sandwich-size Ziploc bag holds about 8 ounces (or 2 cups) of shredded cheese. It's perfect for topping vegetables, salads, and pizzas, or for quick snacks like nachos or quesadillas. Frozen cheese should be used within about six months.

Butter and milk don't require special packaging for the freezer, which makes them very convenient. I freeze packages of butter, then pull out a stick at a time for thawing as needed. If I'm in a hurry, I thaw it in the microwave first. (Take care to remove any metallic-looking wrappers.)

Organization

As with many things, organization is easier said than done. Your organization will depend on the space available and your personality style. I've heard a vicious rumor that there are people in existence who have pantries arranged with military precision. If that's you, you can skip ahead.

For the rest of us, well, we all have the best of intentions. And there are a couple of ways you can go about organizing your canned goods so that there are fewer instances of doubling, running out, or transforming your cabinet into a time capsule.

Some people like to organize foods by color. They put all the greens, reds, yellows, and so on into different sections.

I prefer to organize mine by category, using color as a secondary determinant: vegetables (greens, yellows, and beans separately), meats/fish, soups/chilies/sauces, fruits, and strays such as pickles, hot sauce, and nuts.

Another trick is to try to rotate the newest purchases to the back so that the older ones get used sooner rather than later. Again, easier said than done, but do it when the thought occurs to you.

A LITTLE ABOUT ME

I've never had any formal training as a cook—I simply watched and helped my grandma, a professional cook and wedding caterer, for many years. I suppose she learned by watching and helping her mother, my great-grandma, who supported herself as a boardinghouse cook.

I have very fond memories of going with my grandma on Saturday afternoons to cater weddings in those big kitchens with their giant ovens and vast baking pans. I'm still amazed that she could lift all those large, heavy jars and punch down vats of rising dough. I wondered back then if I would ever know how to make the delicious foods my grandma prepared so effortlessly, without cookbooks.

At the time, helping to cater those weddings was just fun, or a learning activity, or simply lending a hand. I realize now what a wonderfully bonding activity cooking together was.

And I think people today are beginning to realize that again, too. Years ago children had to help out with many household chores because few people had housekeepers, or microwaves, or automatic dishwashers. This was before the words "quality time" laid such a burden at our parents' feet.

I think that somewhere along the line, quality time by definition seemed to exclude any activity that didn't involve the direct disclosure of feelings. I think the pendulum has swung back now, however. Even though we're all strapped for time, on some deep level we know that going about the daily business of life together *is* bonding.

And since we all have to eat, making and eating meals together can be a sort of ritual, a kind of spiritual nourishment, if you will, because preparing food for others is a very nice, very loving thing to do. And it's a way to create good feelings and warm memories. So if you have time to prepare and eat a simple meal together, you have time to bond.

A LITTLE ABOUT THE BOOK

Questions

I've had quite a cadre of testers go through and make all the dishes, so I hope there are no unclear directions. If you're confused by something, you can always e-mail me through my Website at www.canopenergourmet.com. I'll make every effort to get back to you promptly.

Icons and Tools

When I first started cooking for myself after college, I don't know how many times I assembled ingredients for a recipe only to find halfway through that I needed a certain pan or kitchen tool I did not own. I always wished someone would put that information up front, so that's what I've done in my cookbook. There are little icons telling you what's needed for the recipe, as well as a degree-of-difficulty scale based on one, two, or three can openers. I also suggest reading through a recipe first just to be sure. (I never used to do this, but I've learned the hard way that it's worth it.)

Herbs and Spices

I've developed these recipes with maximum convenience and taste in mind, so they are all made with dried herbs and spices. That doesn't mean you have to use them—you may use fresh if you have them on hand. I've included a substitutions guide to help you make conversions to fresh herbs and spices on page 325. The general rule of thumb is that fresh ingredients usually require greater quantities.

Also, be aware that dried herbs and spices can lose their potency over time, so if you consistently find yourself needing to add extra to your recipes, it may be time to restock.

Can Weights

Can weights and volumes may vary a bit by processor and brand—this is perfectly fine. For example, if I call for a 15-ounce can of something, and yours is 14.5, use it. Fractions are not important. If something is 5 whole ounces different (pineapple can be 15 or 20 ounces, for example), then you'll need to make adjustments.

Cooking Times

I usually give approximate cooking times. This is simply because people have different types of ovens (gas or electric) and some can be a few degrees off. I usually give a number that suggests when a dish will be done, or at least when you should start checking. It may need another couple minutes. I just don't want things burning.

Personal Taste

I always tell people to season food the way they like it. I tend to go light on the salt because once you've oversalted something, there's usually no going back. Besides, people should make food they like and like the food they eat. So, experiment if you want to—I won't be offended. And I hope you'll have plenty of helpers in the kitchen to help make your meals a success.

Starters

CHAPTER 2

Indian-Spiced Snack Mix

I think I first had this in London, where a friend's grandma made it regularly (it was called *sev mamra*). It quickly became one of my favorite snacks. This version is a slightly milder one and uses chow mein noodles in place of chickpea noodles, which usually require a trip to an Indian grocery store. Use ⅛ teaspoon of cayenne for the milder version; use ¼ teaspoon for some added fire. Also, don't use white cooking utensils, as turmeric tends to yellow them permanently.

¼ cup cooking oil

⅛ to ¼ teaspoon cayenne

½ teaspoon ground cumin

½ teaspoon ground turmeric

½ teaspoon sugar

¼ teaspoon garlic powder

¼ teaspoon onion powder

¼ teaspoon salt

3 cups crispy puffed rice cereal
(like Rice Krispies®)

1 cup packaged chow mein noodles
(found in the Asian section of most
grocery stores)

1 cup salted peanuts or mixed nuts

1 cup raisins

In a large saucepan or frying pan, heat the oil over low heat just enough to make it hot but not bubbly. While the oil is heating, add the cayenne, cumin, turmeric, sugar, garlic powder, onion powder, and salt. Stir to blend. When the oil gets hot, you should be able to smell some of the spices. At this point, remove pan from the heat and add the puffed rice cereal and chow mein noodles. Stir and toss until coated. Stir in the peanuts and raisins. Let cool to room temperature before storing in an airtight container or Ziploc plastic bag.

Makes about 6 cups

No-Cook Peach Soup

A perfect beginning for a summer evening or special brunch, this simple dish adds a touch of elegance without effort. Canned peaches are so soft that you may use a regular blender or hand blender instead of a food processor. This recipe is a snap to double or triple—great for large gatherings.

Two 15-ounce cans sliced peaches in heavy syrup
1/4 cup bottled lemon juice
1/2 cup sweet white wine, such as Gewürztraminer or white Zinfandel

1/4 teaspoon ground ginger
1/8 teaspoon ground cloves
Pinch dried mint or ground cloves (optional)

Puree the peaches, syrup and all, until they resemble a thin applesauce. Add the remaining ingredients, making sure to stir or process thoroughly. Chill for 1 hour or more before serving. You may want to garnish with a pinch of dried mint leaves or ground cloves in the middle of each bowl of soup.

Makes 3 cups

Italian-Herbed Artichoke Squares

Need something easy, tasty, and impressive? These little squares are super easy and packed with flavor.

Two 6-ounce jars marinated
artichoke hearts, drained

4 eggs

1 tablespoon onion powder

1/2 teaspoon garlic powder

1/2 teaspoon dried basil

1/2 teaspoon dried oregano

1/4 teaspoon salt

1/4 teaspoon ground black pepper

1/4 teaspoon red pepper flakes

2 cups shredded Monterey Jack
cheese

Preheat the oven to 325°F.

Lightly coat an 8 × 8-inch baking pan with oil or nonstick spray. Chop the artichoke hearts into small bite-sized pieces. In a medium-sized bowl, combine the eggs and the onion powder, garlic powder, basil, oregano, salt, black pepper, and red pepper flakes, beating the eggs with a fork or whisk until the spices are blended and the eggs are slightly frothy and lemon-colored. Stir in the chopped artichokes and cheese.

Pour into the prepared pan and bake for 25 to 30 minutes. The dish is ready when it is golden-brown at the edges and set in the middle.

Let cool, then cut into 1-inch squares. (You may want to use toothpicks when serving.) The squares may also be served cold.

Makes sixty-four 1-inch squares

Cheese Tartlets

These make nice little appetizers and are much easier to make than you'd think. Dust them with a pinch of spice for color, if you like.

Refrigerated/frozen dough for a 9-inch pie crust (or use prepackaged frozen tartlet pastries)

2 eggs

1/4 cup milk

3/4 teaspoon onion powder

3/4 cup shredded Swiss, Parmesan, or Cheddar cheese

Dried paprika, basil, oregano, or parsley for color if desired

Preheat the oven to 425°F.

Prepare a 12-cup regular-size muffin tin with oil or nonstick spray to prevent sticking.

Prepare the pie crust as directed if it needs thawing. Cut rounds from the dough using a cookie cutter or the mouth of a drinking glass that's about 3 inches in diameter. Press one circle of dough gently into each muffin mold so that it's centered and the dough comes up around the sides about 1/3 inch or so, making a little cup. (Just eyeball it so that you have sides all the way around.)

You'll need to roll up the extra dough and flatten it again to make the remaining tart circles. (If you don't have a rolling pin, roll a smooth, tall drinking glass instead.) You should have just enough.

In a medium-sized mixing bowl, combine the eggs, milk, and onion powder until smooth. Stir in the cheese, then drop 1 tablespoon of egg mixture into each tart cup.

Bake for about 15 minutes, or until the tops are golden-brown. The tartlets are done when a knife inserted into the center comes out clean. They look really puffy at first, but they settle back down into tarts as they cool. Dust with suggested spices, if desired.

Makes 12

Shrimp Cocktail

This is a great appetizer to make ahead of time, as chilling it in the refrigerator only enhances the flavor.

1 cup ketchup

2 tablespoons prepared horseradish

1 teaspoon balsamic vinegar

1 teaspoon Worcestershire sauce

1/2 teaspoon onion powder

1/8 teaspoon salt

1/8 teaspoon sugar

Pinch cayenne or hot pepper sauce
(optional)

One 4-ounce can tiny shrimp,
drained

In a small mixing bowl, whisk together everything but the shrimp. Gently stir in the shrimp. Chill for 1 hour or more in the refrigerator before serving.

Serves 4

Smoked Salmon Pâté

This is an easy yet elegant starter that appears to be far more trouble than it is. If you cannot find canned smoked salmon in your grocery store, stir 3 teaspoons of Liquid Smoke® into regular canned salmon.

¼ cup mayonnaise

1 teaspoon onion powder

One 6.5-ounce can smoked salmon, drained

In a small bowl or other container, combine the mayonnaise and onion powder. Add the salmon, then puree with a hand blender or food processor. (It purees very quickly.)

Mold or serve in a small bowl with crackers, sliced baguette, or cocktail rye bread.

Makes about 1 cup

Shrimp Dip

This is a great dip to make ahead, as chilling in the refrigerator only enhances its flavor. By the way, you can soften the cream cheese by heating it, unwrapped, in the microwave on medium for about 15 seconds. This is the method I use, as there's something about leaving a dairy product on the counter for an hour that just gives me the willies.

8 ounces cream cheese, softened

$^1/_2$ cup sour cream

1 tablespoon Worcestershire sauce

1 teaspoon onion powder

$^1/_4$ teaspoon garlic powder

$^1/_4$ teaspoon cayenne

Two 4-ounce cans tiny or broken shrimp, drained

In a large bowl, combine the cream cheese, sour cream, Worcestershire sauce, onion powder, garlic powder, and cayenne. Stir in the shrimp. Cover and chill for a couple hours or more before serving.

Makes about 1 $^1/_2$ cups

VARIATION

Curried Shrimp Dip

Follow the recipe for Shrimp Dip above, adding $^1/_4$ to $^1/_2$ teaspoon of curry powder.

Smoked Oyster and Bacon Dip

As with other "softened" cream cheese recipes, if you don't want to wait an hour for the cream cheese to soften, unwrap it and place it in the microwave on medium for 15 to 20 seconds; it makes this tasty dip a snap to put together. This appetizer works equally well for holidays, parties, or unexpected drop-in guests. You can also use low-fat cheese to trim calories. Just make sure you use real bottled bacon *pieces,* not bacon bits or chips.

One 3.75-ounce tin smoked oyster
   pieces (see Note)
One 8-ounce package cream cheese,
   softened

1/2 teaspoon onion powder
1 tablespoon Worcestershire sauce
1/8 teaspoon salt
1/4 cup bottled real bacon pieces

Chop the oysters fine. In a small to medium mixing bowl, combine the oysters with the cream cheese and blend well. Add the onion powder, Worcestershire sauce, and salt, then blend again. Stir in the bacon pieces. Chill for 1 hour. Try serving with hearty wheat crackers.

Makes about 1 1/4 cups

Note: If you have difficulty with the tin key, try using a manual can opener.

Tarragon Tuna Dip

One thing I've learned about dried herbs and spices is that their flavor can fade a little if you've had them a while. It seems to me that tarragon is particularly prone to this, so do a taste test before you get started.

One 6-ounce can tuna, drained and flaked

1 teaspoon prepared horseradish

1 cup sour cream (low- or nonfat works well, too)

1 teaspoon onion powder

1/4 teaspoon salt

1 teaspoon Worcestershire sauce

1 teaspoon dried tarragon (or to taste)

In a small or medium mixing bowl, combine the tuna and horseradish. Add the sour cream and stir. Add the onion powder, salt, Worcestershire, and tarragon, and mix well. Chill for 1 hour, then serve with chips, crackers, or vegetables.

Makes about 1 1/4 cups

Mediterranean White Bean Dip

If you like hummus, you'll probably like this. It's fast, low in fat, and nutritious. And the beans are easier to mash than garbanzo beans (used in hummus)—I use a hand blender, but you could easily use a fork or the back of a spoon.

One 15-ounce can small white beans,
   rinsed and drained
1 tablespoon olive oil
1/2 teaspoon bottled lemon juice
1/2 teaspoon garlic powder
1/4 teaspoon onion powder

1/4 teaspoon dried basil
1/4 teaspoon dried oregano
1/8 to 1/4 teaspoon salt (see Note)
1/8 to 1/4 teaspoon black pepper (see
   Note)

In a medium-sized mixing bowl, mash the beans until they're of a dipping consistency. Add the remaining ingredients and mix thoroughly. Serve with crackers, chips, vegetables, or toasted pita wedges.

Makes 1 cup

Note: Use 1/8 teaspoon each salt and pepper if your dippers are on the bland side—for instance, unseasoned pita wedges or water crackers. Use 1/4 teaspoon otherwise, bearing in mind that the dip alone will probably taste too salty but will be just fine on salted crackers, vegetables, and so on.

Cajun Cheese Dip

Don't let all the spices listed here scare you off—most people have them on hand. I've limited the "fire factor" here so that you can serve it to a wide variety of people, but I've given you the option of raising it to a three-alarm dip. (Please be sure to use garlic and onion *powder,* not salt.) And there will be enough of the spice mixture you create to make two batches of dip.

1 teaspoon garlic powder	1/4 teaspoon sugar
1 teaspoon onion powder	1/4 teaspoon salt
1 teaspoon ground black pepper	1/8–1/4 teaspoon cayenne
1 teaspoon paprika	One 8-ounce package cream cheese,
1/2 teaspoon chili powder	softened (see Note)

In a small bowl, whisk together the garlic and onion powders, pepper, paprika, chili powder, sugar, salt, and cayenne. In another small or medium mixing bowl, combine 1 tablespoon of the spice mixture with the cream cheese and blend well.

Serve with crackers or vegetables.

Makes about 1 1/2 cups

Note: You may soften cream cheese by heating it unwrapped in the microwave for 15 to 20 seconds.

Pesto-Cheese Spread

This is one of my favorites and is a great make-ahead dish. It's simple and tasty. It's also perfect for holiday get-togethers, with its slight emerald hue. Consider using leftover pesto as a pizza or pasta sauce.

Two 8-ounce packages cream cheese, at room temperature
1 tablespoon prepared pesto sauce (more if desired)

1 cup salted chopped nuts, such as pine nuts, walnuts, or almonds (optional)

If the cream cheese is not at room temperature, remove it from its packaging and microwave it 15 to 20 seconds.

In a medium mixing bowl, combine the cream cheese and pesto sauce until smooth. You may serve immediately, or:

Line a 4 × 8-inch bread tin or cake pan with plastic wrap. Press cheese spread into the pan and then wrap it in plastic wrap. Chill in the refrigerator for at least 3 hours to firm (or 1 hour in the freezer). Unwrap to serve. If desired, coat the cheese bar with chopped nuts, pressing them gently into the cheese.

Serve with crackers or raw vegetables.

Makes sixteen 1-ounce servings

Sun-Dried Tomato and Cheese Spread

This, too, is very simple and is great on crackers or bagels. Consider doubling the recipe and molding it in a heart-shaped pan for Valentine's Day.

Two 8-ounce packages cream cheese, at room temperature
3 tablespoons prepared sun-dried tomato spread/sauce (or more if desired)

1 cup salted chopped nuts, such as pine nuts, walnuts, or almonds (optional)

If the cream cheese is not at room temperature, remove it from its packaging and microwave it for 15 to 20 seconds.

In a medium mixing bowl, combine the cream cheese and sun-dried tomato sauce until smooth. You may serve immediately, or:

Line a 4 × 8-inch bread tin or cake pan with plastic wrap. Press the cheese spread into the pan, then wrap it with the plastic. Chill in the refrigerator for at least 3 hours to firm (or 1 hour in the freezer). Unwrap to serve. If desired, coat the cheese bar with chopped nuts, pressing them gently into the cheese.

Serve with crackers, bagels, or raw vegetables.

Makes sixteen 1-ounce servings

Cream Cheese and Mango Chutney Appetizer

This is an instant appetizer, appropriate for many occasions. One of my testers liked this recipe topped with tiny shrimp (which also come in cans). Remember that if you prefer not to wait for the cream cheese to soften, you may unwrap it and heat it in the microwave for about 15 seconds to speed the process. Zap it again if needed.

**One 8-ounce package cream cheese,
softened** (low-fat okay)
**Approximately half an 8-ounce jar
mango chutney**

**Crackers and vegetables for
dipping**

Place unwrapped block of cream cheese on a serving plate. Spread about half the jar (or more) of chutney on top of the cream cheese, forming a layer about 1/2-inch thick. It's okay if some chutney drips down the sides. Serve with crackers or raw vegetables.

Serves 4 to 6

Faux Guacamole

Whether you're just out of avocados or you're looking for a way to slim down this Mexican favorite, you'll have to give this recipe a try sometime. I stumbled on it while I was trying to make split pea soup—it tasted nothing like split pea soup but reminded me a lot of guacamole. Later, I learned that others have used peas as an avocado substitute as well because they are a low-fat source of protein.

One 15-ounce can very young small
    sweet peas, drained
1/4 cup sour cream
1/2 cup prepared salsa
2 teaspoons bottled lime or lemon
    juice

1/2 teaspoon onion powder
1/2 teaspoon dried cilantro
1/4 teaspoon salt
1/4 teaspoon ground cumin
1/4 teaspoon garlic powder
1/8 teaspoon cayenne (optional)

In a small mixing bowl, mash the peas with a potato masher or fork, or process them with a hand blender or food processor. Don't overprocess; some texture is good. Add the remaining ingredients and stir until blended.

Consider serving with tortilla chips, canned sliced olives, sour cream, or shredded Cheddar cheese.

Makes about 2 cups

Red Pepper Jam

This jam goes wonderfully on top of cream cheese and crackers or onion bagels. Make it well ahead of serving time so that it's good and chilled. You might think about giving it around the holidays as something different in a basket or stocking. One 12-ounce jar of red peppers is enough for this recipe.

¼ cup pureed roasted red peppers from a jar	2 tablespoons mild canned diced chilies
¼ cup diced roasted red peppers from a jar	¼ cup sugar
¼ cup balsamic vinegar	2 tablespoons cornstarch dissolved in a little cold water

Prepare the peppers, then combine them in a medium nonreactive saucepan with vinegar, chilies, 2 tablespoons water, and sugar. Bring to a boil, then add cornstarch dissolved in cold water. Stir for about 3 minutes or until the pepper mixture has a thick, custard-like consistency.

Remove from the heat and let cool at least ten minutes, then pour it into a sealed glass container. Cover and chill for at least three hours, preferably overnight.

Serve on onion bagels with cream cheese, crackers, toast sticks, etc. Great for a Southwestern-themed meal.

Makes about 1 cup

Salads

CHAPTER 3

Pineapple-Orange Salad

This is an easy fruit salad that doesn't require dressing. Perfect during the summer when you want something cool, it's also great for a winter pick-me-up. The textures of the pineapples and oranges hold up very well, making them seem more like fresh fruit.

One 15- or 20-ounce can chunk pineapple, drained
One 15-ounce can mandarin oranges, drained

One 15-ounce can dark pitted *sweet* Bing cherries, drained

In a medium-sized serving bowl, combine all of the drained fruit and toss gently. Serve at once or chill and serve later.

Serves 8

Quick Potato Salad

If your potatoes have already been cleaned, peeled, and boiled for you, potato salad turns out to be pretty easy to make.

Two 15-ounce cans whole white
    potatoes, rinsed and drained
1 cup mayonnaise
1 teaspoon rice vinegar
1 teaspoon onion powder
1/2 teaspoon sugar
2/3 cup chopped sweet pickle (about
    4 small ones) or 2/3 cup sweet relish

1 1/4 teaspoons celery salt
One 8-ounce can sliced water
    chestnuts, rinsed and drained
2 hard-boiled eggs, chopped (optional)
One 2.25-ounce can sliced olives,
    drained (optional)
Salt and pepper

Chop the potatoes into bite-sized pieces and set aside. In a medium-sized mixing bowl, combine the mayonnaise with the vinegar, onion powder, and sugar. Add the potatoes and chopped pickle or relish.

Sprinkle the celery salt over the water chestnuts and toss, then add them to the potato-mayonnaise mixture. Add the chopped eggs and olives if desired. Toss everything to coat, then salt and pepper as desired. Keep chilled. (This salad tastes better after it's been left to chill, as the flavors ripen.)

Serves 6

Chinese Chicken Salad

This easy, summery salad is just perfect for lunch or as a first course for dinner. Consider serving it with a side of coconut rice.

Lettuce for four to six people (about one 16-ounce package, with carrots if possible)

One 8-ounce package chopped cabbage

One 10-ounce can white chunk chicken, rinsed and drained

¹/₂ teaspoon ground ginger

Two 11-ounce cans mandarin oranges, drained, juice reserved

Chow mein noodles (about three-quarters of a 6-ounce package)

Dressing

¹/₂ cup peanut or other cooking oil

¹/₄ cup rice vinegar

1 teaspoon mayonnaise

1 teaspoon sugar

1 teaspoon soy sauce

In a large mixing bowl, combine the lettuce and cabbage. Sprinkle the chicken with ginger, toss to coat, and add to the lettuce mixture. Add the oranges and noodles, and toss everything together.

To make the dressing: Combine the oil, vinegar, ¼ cup of mandarin orange syrup, mayonnaise, sugar, and soy sauce. Whisk until the oil and vinegar combine (you may want to use a hand blender). Add the dressing to the salad and toss, or dress each serving separately.

Serves 4 to 6

Chicken Caesar Salad

A traditional Caesar salad isn't as hard to make as you might think, if you use a few shortcuts. Keep packaged croutons on hand and the hardest part is done for you. In a pinch, you can substitute turkey or tuna for the chicken.

Chicken

One 6.5-ounce can white chunk chicken, rinsed and drained (press to expel excess moisture)

1 teaspoon bottled lemon juice

1/4 teaspoon garlic powder

1/4 teaspoon onion powder

1/4 cup real shredded Parmesan cheese (*not* the powdered kind)

Dressing

1/2 cup olive oil

2 anchovy fillets from a 2-ounce tin, chopped fine or mashed

2 tablespoons bottled lemon juice

1/2 teaspoon garlic powder

1/2 teaspoon onion powder

1/4 teaspoon dry mustard

One 10-ounce package torn romaine

1/2 cup real shredded Parmesan cheese (*not* the powdered kind)

1 cup packaged croutons

Combine the chicken with the lemon juice, garlic powder, and onion powder, and mix well. Add the Parmesan cheese and toss to coat.

For the dressing, whisk together the olive oil, anchovy fillets, lemon juice, garlic powder, onion powder, and mustard until thickened.

Place the salad greens in a large serving bowl. Pour the dressing over them. Add the chicken mixture, Parmesan cheese, and croutons. Toss to coat.

Serves 4 to 6

Pineapple-Ham Tossed Salad

This salad makes for good summertime eating—nothing to heat and plenty of crunch. Serve it with your favorite Oriental salad dressing, make a basic vinaigrette using rice vinegar (page 233), or use Grandma's Salad Dressing (page 238).

Two 5-ounce cans ham, drained

One 8-ounce can water chestnuts, drained

One 16-ounce can bean sprouts, drained

One 16- or 20-ounce can chunk pineapple, drained

1 cup cashews or slivered almonds

Lettuce for four people (preferably something with a little cabbage and carrot)

Salad dressing of choice

Dice the ham and chop the water chestnuts. Combine them in a medium-sized mixing bowl with the bean sprouts, pineapple, nuts, and lettuce. Toss, and serve with salad dressing.

Serves 4

Salmon-Orange Salad with Ginger-Lime Dressing

Here's a salmon salad with a little bit of an Asian spin. Terrific for spring or summer lunches.

One 15-ounce can salmon

One 8-ounce can water chestnuts, drained

1 tablespoon plus 1 teaspoon sherry (optional)

1/2 cup mayonnaise

2 teaspoons ground ginger

Lettuce for four people

Two 11-ounce cans mandarin oranges, drained

1/2 cup slivered or chopped almonds

Ginger-Lime Dressing (recipe follows)

Drain the salmon and, if desired, remove the skin and bones (though it's not necessary and they contain much calcium). Place the salmon in a medium-sized mixing bowl. Coarsely chop the water chestnuts and add them to the salmon. If you're using sherry, combine it with the mayonnaise; if not, simply combine the mayonnaise with the salmon mixture. Add the ginger and stir well.

To serve, place a scoop of salmon salad on a mound of lettuce, then sprinkle with mandarin oranges and almonds. Add dressing as desired.

Serves 4

Ginger-Lime Dressing

$1/2$ cup peanut or other cooking oil

$1/4$ cup rice vinegar

2 teaspoons sugar

1 teaspoon ground ginger

$1/2$ teaspoon soy sauce

Whisk together all of the ingredients until thickened.

Serves 4

Tuna Salad with Pesto Mayonnaise

Here's a little twist on an old favorite: pesto sauce. It's a nice change from the old routine. Use it for sandwiches, or put a scoop on a bed of lettuce dressed with a basic vinaigrette (page 233).

^{1}/4 cup mayonnaise

^{1}/4 cup pesto sauce from a jar

One 8-ounce can water chestnuts, drained

Two 6-ounce cans tuna, drained

^{1}/2 cup chopped or slivered almonds

In a small mixing bowl, blend the mayonnaise with the pesto sauce. Coarsely chop the water chestnuts. Add the chestnuts, tuna, and almonds to the pesto mayonnaise and mix thoroughly.

Serves 6

Corn, Red Pepper, and Cheese Salad

When it's hot out, sometimes a salad hits the spot, and this one doesn't heat up the house when you're making it.

Two 15-ounce cans corn, drained
2/3 cup chopped roasted red peppers
    from a jar
One 4-ounce can mild diced chilies,
    drained
1/2 pound Jack cheese, cut into cubes

1/3 cup olive oil or other cooking oil
1/4 cup rice vinegar
1 teaspoon dried oregano
1/8 teaspoon salt
Extra salt and pepper

In a medium-sized mixing bowl, combine the corn, chopped red peppers, chilies, and Jack cheese cubes. In a small bowl, whisk together the oil, vinegar, oregano, and salt. Pour over the corn mixture and toss to coat. Add extra salt and pepper if desired. You may serve immediately, or chill to serve later.

Serves 8

Corn and Kidney Bean Salad

This is one of my favorite instant salads. It's not only delicious, it delivers solid nutrition (grain and legume, giving you the whole amino-acid chain for protein), and it's pretty, too. This one travels well, so it's ideal for picnics or potlucks.

One 15-ounce can dark red kidney beans, rinsed and drained

One 15-ounce can corn, drained

3 tablespoons olive oil or other cooking oil

2 tablespoons rice vinegar

Combine the beans with the corn in a small mixing bowl. Whisk together the oil and vinegar, then drizzle over the corn-and-bean mixture. Toss to coat. Serve at room temperature or chill to serve cold.

Serves 6

Corn and Tomato Salad

This makes a nice side dish for Mexican or Southwestern fare.

One 15-ounce can diced tomatoes in juice, drained

One 15-ounce can corn, drained

3 tablespoons olive oil or other cooking oil

2 tablespoons rice vinegar

Combine the tomatoes with the corn in a small mixing bowl. Whisk together the oil and vinegar, then drizzle over the corn-and-tomato mixture. Toss to coat. Serve at room temperature or chill to serve cold.

Serves 6

Chickpea, Tomato, and Olive Salad with Lemon-Basil Vinaigrette

I use whole tomatoes, as opposed to diced, in this recipe because I think they work better aesthetically in larger pieces. In a pinch, however, you can use diced tomatoes. When draining the tomatoes, you should know that they seem to have a bottomless well of juice. Just drain them as best you can, and then before you add the dressing to the salad, drain any extra juice. Also, chickpeas and garbanzo beans are actually the same thing, they just have different names in different regions of the country.

One 15-ounce can chickpeas/ garbanzo beans, rinsed and drained

One 28-ounce can (or two 14.5-ounce cans) whole peeled tomatoes, drained

One 6-ounce can whole pitted black olives, drained

Vinaigrette

1/2 cup olive oil

1/4 cup rice vinegar

1 tablespoon bottled lemon juice

1/2 teaspoon dried basil

1/2 teaspoon dried oregano

1/8 teaspoon salt

Empty the chickpeas into a medium-sized mixing bowl. Cut the tomatoes into fairly good sized chunks (basically into quarters), and add them to the bowl. Slice the olives in half before adding them to the bowl. Toss together.

For the vinaigrette, combine all of the ingredients and mix well. Pour out any tomato juice that may have accumulated in the mixing bowl, then add the vinaigrette and toss to coat.

Serves 6

Green Bean and Beet Salad

This would make a colorful addition to a holiday table. It's also easy to take along to potlucks or picnics. Serve as is or on a mound of lettuce.

One 15-ounce can sliced or julienne-cut beets, drained

One 15-ounce can green beans, drained

3 tablespoons olive oil

2 tablespoons rice vinegar

Lettuce for 6, if desired

If using sliced beets, chop them into quarters (they're usually stacked, and they slice very easily). Place the beets and beans in a medium-sized mixing bowl. Whisk together the oil and vinegar until well blended, then pour over the beans and beets. Serve at once, alone or on a mound of lettuce, or chill and serve later.

Serves 6

Soups

CHAPTER 4

Cream of Artichoke Soup

This soup makes a great starter course for a nice dinner. Have Parmesan cheese on hand to sprinkle on top as a garnish, if desired. Please be aware that some companies preserve their artichokes with vinegar; for this dish you want artichoke *bottoms* (not hearts) preserved using salt *without* vinegar.

**Two 14.5-ounce cans artichoke
    bottoms, without added vinegar**
One 14.5-ounce can chicken broth
One 12-ounce can evaporated milk
2 teaspoons onion powder
1/2 teaspoon sugar
**1/8 teaspoon ground white or black
    pepper**

Salt
**2 tablespoons cornstarch dissolved
    in a little cold water** (optional)
**Real grated Parmesan cheese for
    garnish** (*not* the powdered kind;
    optional)

Drain the artichokes, then puree them and put them in a medium-sized saucepan. (If you're using a hand blender, you can puree them right in the saucepan.) Add the chicken broth, milk, onion powder, sugar, pepper, salt to taste, and cornstarch mixture (if using), and cook over medium heat until hot (see Note). Sprinkle individual servings with Parmesan cheese, if desired.

Serves 4

Note: If using cornstarch, bring soup to a boil and stir until thickened.

Minted Cream of Asparagus Soup

Asparagus makes a lovely soup, just perfect as an appetizer or with a sandwich at lunch. This soup is appropriate for any season, but the mint lends itself nicely to spring or fall occasions. Asparagus is fairly low in calories, and you can shave off even more of them by using nonfat evaporated milk in this dish.

2 cubes chicken or vegetable bouillon

Two 14.5-ounce cans asparagus spears and tips

One 12-ounce can evaporated milk

3 tablespoons cornstarch dissolved in a little cold water

1 1/2 teaspoons onion powder

1/2 teaspoon salt

1/4 teaspoon garlic powder

1/4 teaspoon bottled lemon juice

1 tablespoon dried mint

Additional salt and pepper

In a medium saucepan, combine the bouillon with 2 cups of water and set over medium-high heat to dissolve. Meanwhile, drain both cans of asparagus and puree.

When the bouillon has dissolved, stir in the pureed asparagus, milk, and cornstarch mixture. Blend in the remaining ingredients and bring to a low boil, stirring until thickened. Add more salt and pepper if desired.

Serves 6

Minted Cream of Asparagus Soup with Ham

Follow the recipe above, and add one 5-ounce can of ham, drained and diced, with the last ingredients.

Cream of Chicken Soup
with Mushrooms and Almonds

This soup makes a delicious first course or side dish for many meals. The recipe can easily be doubled for larger quantities.

One 10.5-ounce can condensed cream of chicken soup
One 12-ounce can evaporated milk (nonfat is okay)
One 7-ounce can sliced mushrooms
2 to 3 tablespoons white wine or sherry (optional)

Pinch ground nutmeg
3 tablespoons coarsely chopped almonds
Salt and pepper
Dried parsley for garnish (optional)

In a medium saucepan, combine the soup with the milk and place over medium heat, stirring periodically. Drain and coarsely chop the mushrooms, then add them to the soup mixture. Add the wine, if using, and the nutmeg. Bring the soup to a boil.

Serve with a garnish of 1 tablespoon chopped almonds for each bowl. Salt and pepper as desired. Add a pinch of dried parsley to the middle of each soup bowl, if using.

Serves 3

Cream of Chicken Soup with Mushrooms, Almonds, and Extra Chicken

To add more protein to this soup, follow the recipe above and add one 6-ounce can of chicken (rinsed, drained, and flaked) to the mushroom step.

Cream of Pumpkin Soup

This is an ideal savory starter for a holiday meal. It doesn't even require puree-ing, which gives you more time for other things. Pumpkin is loaded with vitamin A and has a relatively low calorie content—about 40 calories per serving, according to my label. Use nonfat evaporated milk and you've got a low-calorie soup course with no one the wiser.

One 15-ounce can pumpkin (*not* pumpkin pie filling)
One 14.5-ounce can chicken broth
One 12-ounce can evaporated milk
1/2 teaspoon onion powder

1/4 teaspoon garlic powder
1/4 teaspoon salt (or to taste)
1/8 teaspoon ground black pepper (or to taste)
1/8 teaspoon ground nutmeg

Combine all of the ingredients in a saucepan. Stir over medium heat until well blended and hot.

Serves 5

Spinach Soup

This is a mild-flavored soup, so even if you don't typically care for spinach, you may find that you like this soup after all.

One 15-ounce can spinach

One 14.5-ounce can chicken broth

One 12-ounce can evaporated milk

1/2 teaspoon rice vinegar

1/2 teaspoon onion powder

1/4 teaspoon salt

1/8 teaspoon ground nutmeg

1 tablespoon cornstarch dissolved in
   a little cold water (optional)

Thoroughly rinse and drain the spinach in a colander or sieve, expelling as much moisture as possible. Combine the spinach, chicken broth, and milk, then puree with a hand blender or blender until smooth. Place the mixture in a saucepan over medium-high heat. Add the vinegar, onion powder, salt, nutmeg, and cornstarch, if using. Bring to a boil, stirring often. The soup is ready when it has reached a boil, or when it has thickened (if you're using cornstarch).

Serves 4

Black Bean and Corn Chowder

This soup can be a meal unto itself, since it combines a grain with a legume. For a thicker soup, add cornstarch as directed below. For a Southwestern flair, consider adding a can of diced chilies.

Two 15-ounce cans cream-style corn

One 12-ounce can evaporated milk
   (low-fat is okay)

One 15-ounce can black beans,
   rinsed and drained

1 tablespoon onion powder

1/2 teaspoon salt

1/4 teaspoon ground black pepper

One 4-ounce can diced chilies
   (optional)

1 to 2 tablespoons cornstarch
   dissolved in a little cold water
   (optional)

Place the corn, milk, 12 ounces (one milk can) of water, beans, onion powder, salt, pepper, and chilies (if using) in a medium-sized saucepan and cook over medium heat. Stir occasionally until hot and steaming, at which point you may serve, or add dissolved cornstarch. If using cornstarch, cook for another minute or two until the soup thickens, then serve.

Serves 6

White Bean Soup

You can use any type of white beans for this soup. Some labels read "small white beans," while others are called cannellini beans or navy beans. Either way, you're getting a low-fat source of protein and fiber. And there's something warm and satisfying about hot bean soup during the winter months.

Two 15-ounce cans white beans

One 14.5-ounce can chicken broth

1/2 teaspoon onion powder

1/4 teaspoon garlic powder

Salt and pepper

Do not rinse or drain the beans. Puree all but 1/2 cup of the beans, until they have a consistency like refried beans (some whole beans, some pureed). Combine the pureed beans, whole beans, and chicken broth in a medium saucepan and stir over medium heat. Season with onion powder, garlic powder, and salt and pepper if desired. The soup is ready when it begins to boil.

Serves 4

Potato Chowder

This is a nice soup to whip up on a cold night. It's fast and very hearty. Adding ham to it makes it nearly a meal unto itself.

One 12-ounce can evaporated milk
   plus a can full of water (or
   substitute 3 cups whole milk)
1 tablespoon butter
Two 15-ounce cans sliced potatoes,
   rinsed and drained
2 teaspoons onion powder

3/4 teaspoon salt
1/2 teaspoon celery salt
1/4 teaspoon ground black pepper
1/4 teaspoon garlic powder
1/4 cup cornstarch dissolved in a
   little cold water
Salt and pepper

Place the evaporated milk and water (or whole milk) and butter in a medium-sized saucepan over medium heat. While the milk is heating, dice the potatoes. Add them to the milk, then add the remaining ingredients. Bring to a low boil and stir until thickened (just a minute or two after it reaches a boil). Taste and add more salt and pepper if desired.

Serves 5

Potato Chowder with Ham

To the above recipe, add one 5-ounce can of ham, rinsed and diced, at the potato step.

Cheesy Potato Chowder

To the recipe for Potato Chowder, add 1 cup of shredded Cheddar cheese at the end. Cook until melted.

Manhattan Clam Chowder

This is a simple yet tasty soup that can serve as a starter or a meal. Great with seasoned oyster crackers.

5 cubes vegetable bouillon

One 15-ounce can sliced potatoes, rinsed and drained

One 15-ounce can diced tomatoes, drained

Two or three 6-ounce cans chopped clams, *not drained*

1/4 teaspoon salt

1/8 teaspoon ground black pepper

Place 4 cups of water in a medium saucepan, add the bouillon cubes, and heat. Meanwhile, chop the rinsed potatoes into bite-sized pieces. Add the potatoes and the remaining ingredients to the bouillon mixture. Bring to a boil. Season with more salt and ground black pepper if desired.

Serves 6

Salmon Chowder

Here's another way to use canned salmon. This is lovely on a winter night, or serve it with salad for a nice lunch. Remember that you don't have to remove any skin and bones you find in the salmon—they have lots of calcium and vitamins and are quite soft. (However, I usually remove them for aesthetic reasons.)

One 12-ounce can evaporated milk plus an equal can of water (or substitute 3 cups whole milk)

1 tablespoon butter

Two 15-ounce cans sliced potatoes, rinsed and drained

2 teaspoons onion powder

3/4 teaspoon salt

1/2 teaspoon celery salt

1/2 teaspoon Worcestershire sauce

1/4 teaspoon ground black pepper

1/4 teaspoon garlic powder

One 6-ounce can salmon or smoked salmon, drained, skin and bones removed if desired

1/4 cup cornstarch dissolved in a little cold water

Place the milk and water (or whole milk) and butter over medium heat in a medium-sized saucepan. While the milk is heating, dice the potatoes. Add them to the milk, then add the remaining ingredients. Bring to a low boil and stir until thickened (just a minute or two after it reaches a boil).

Serves 5

Shrimp Bisque

The shrimp in this dish gives the soup a nice subtle coral color. It's a snap to put together and an easy way to add a touch of elegance to dinner. I always use the tiny broken shrimp because they're going to be pureed anyway, and they're often available at those "everything's a dollar" type stores.

One 6-ounce can tiny (or broken) shrimp

One 10.75-ounce can condensed cream of celery soup

One 12-ounce can evaporated milk

1/8 teaspoon each salt and pepper (optional)

Drain the shrimp, then puree them (I do this right in the saucepan). Combine with the remaining ingredients in a medium-sized saucepan. Stir over medium heat until blended and hot.

Serves 3

Cheesy Tuna Chowder

This is nearly instant-gratification comfort food, and it goes down warm on a cold winter night. Upgrade your meal by pouring a nice dry white wine to accompany it. (You may even want to splash a couple of tablespoons of wine into the soup.) You can shave off calories by using nonfat evaporated milk.

One 15-ounce can whole potatoes, rinsed and drained

One 10.75-ounce can Cheddar cheese soup

One 12-ounce can evaporated milk

One 6-ounce can chunk white tuna, rinsed and drained

¼ teaspoon ground black pepper (optional)

Chop the potatoes into bite-sized pieces. In a medium saucepan, combine the potatoes, cheese soup, and milk, stirring over medium heat. Add the tuna, then add pepper, if desired. Bring to a boil and serve hot.

Serves 4

Sweet Potato Soup

Sweet potatoes are another vegetable with lots of beta-carotene. Whip up this yummy soup in the fall or winter. It makes a nice addition to holiday fare.

**One 29-ounce can cut sweet potatoes
or yams**
Two 14.5-ounce cans chicken broth
1 teaspoon onion powder

¼ teaspoon ground nutmeg
¼ teaspoon ground black pepper
¼ teaspoon salt (optional)

Drain the sweet potatoes, reserving ¼ cup syrup. Place sweet potatoes in a blender with one can of chicken broth (or use a hand blender) and puree until smooth. Place sweet potato puree in a medium-sized saucepan over medium heat. Stir in remaining chicken broth, reserved syrup, and all other ingredients. Heat to boiling and serve.

Serves 4

Black-Eyed Pea Soup

Beans are a great source of low-fat protein and fiber. Here's a simple soup, very low in fat, but loaded with flavor.

Two 15-ounce cans black-eyed peas

One 14.5-ounce can chicken broth

1$^{1}/_{2}$ teaspoons onion powder

1 teaspoon garlic powder

$^{1}/_{4}$ teaspoon salt

$^{1}/_{8}$ to $^{1}/_{4}$ teaspoon ground black pepper

One 5-ounce can ham, drained and chopped (optional)

Puree one can of black-eyed peas with its liquid. Drain the second can of peas, then combine all ingredients in a medium saucepan. Heat to boiling, stirring periodically.

Serves 4

Grandma's Vegetable Soup

This is adapted from one of my grandma's own soup recipes. One of the great things about it is that you use the juice the vegetables come in, so no nutrients are lost.

1 cup small macaroni, rice, or barley

One 15-ounce can whole potatoes, drained

One 15-ounce can beef broth plus two equal cans of water

One 7-ounce can sliced mushrooms, drained

One 15-ounce can sliced carrots, *not* drained

One 15-ounce can diced tomatoes, *not* drained

One 15-ounce can spicy (or "Texas Ranch Style") beans, *not* drained

2 tablespoons butter

1 tablespoon (or 3 cubes/teaspoons) beef bouillon powder

1 tablespoon onion powder

1 tablespoon dried parsley

2 teaspoons sugar

1 teaspoon chili powder

1 teaspoon garlic powder

1 teaspoon salt

Additional salt and pepper

Cook the macaroni, rice, or barley according to the package directions.

Chop the potatoes into bite-sized pieces. Place the potatoes, along with all of the other ingredients except the macaroni, in a large saucepan and bring to a boil. (Make sure to pay attention to which cans are drained and which are not.)

When the macaroni has cooked, add it to the soup. Serve whenever it's nice and hot. Add extra salt and pepper if desired.

Serves 8

VARIATION

Homemade Vegetable-Beef Soup

To the recipe above, add two 12-ounce cans roast beef in gravy, not *drained, at any time.*

Gazpacho

This soup makes a wonderful starter or side for a summer evening meal—you don't even need a stove top. You should make it ahead of time and let it chill for several hours, though it's also very good at room temperature. (To cheat and speed the chilling process, I often put foods that need chilling in the freezer for about an hour.) Feel free to add other canned ingredients as well: chopped carrots, corn, olives, garbanzo beans, cannellini beans, chopped red bell pepper, etc.

One 46-ounce can vegetable-tomato juice (such as V-8®)
One 15-ounce can diced tomatoes with juice
One 4-ounce can mild chopped diced chilies, drained

1 cup mild prepared salsa
1 teaspoon Worcestershire sauce
1 teaspoon bottled lime or lemon juice

Combine all of the ingredients in a large mixing bowl. Cover and chill. Serve with croutons if desired.

Serves 8

Borscht

This is a nontraditional way to make the famous Russian beet soup, borscht. It's quite simple, and loaded with beta-carotenes.

Four 14.5-ounce cans beef broth

One 15-ounce can beets, drained and chopped

One 14.5-ounce can crispy sauerkraut, drained (see Note)

One 14.5-ounce can whole onions, drained

One 15-ounce can sliced carrots, drained

Salt and black pepper to taste

Sour cream, for garnish

Combine all ingredients in a large saucepan and heat to boiling. Serve hot with a dollop of sour cream as a garnish.

Serves 8 to 10

Note: You may chop the sauerkraut if desired.

Borscht with Beef

To make this soup a complete meal, add two 12-ounce cans of roast beef with gravy (drained) to the pan.

Meat and Poultry

CHAPTER 5

Southwestern Beef Stew

This is one of those recipes that's perfect when 5:00 P.M. rolls around and you're thinking, "I have no idea what I'm making for dinner." Frankly, that's how I came up with it, too. Now it's one of my favorites because it's tasty, and it combines meat and vegetables for a whole meal. You may want to serve it with warm tortillas on the side. (You can find enchilada sauce in the grocery store in the Mexican food section, near the chilies and salsas, or you may make your own using the recipe found on page 252.)

One 15-ounce can sliced potatoes, rinsed and drained

One 15-ounce can prepared enchilada sauce or 2 cups homemade sauce

Two 12-ounce cans roast beef with gravy, drained

One 15-ounce can corn, drained, or hominy, rinsed and drained

1 cup chopped roasted red peppers from a jar

Chop or break the potatoes into manageable pieces for eating. Put the potatoes in a saucepan with the enchilada sauce over medium heat. Add the roast beef, corn or hominy, and roasted red peppers. Heat to boiling, then lower the heat and simmer for 10 minutes. (You may simmer it longer, but give it at least 10 minutes to let the flavors steep.)

Serves 4

Homemade Chili

I've noticed that some brands of ready-made chili contain additives. What I like about this recipe is that I know exactly what's in it because I put it there. Serve this with cornbread (page 145) for a hearty meal.

Two 15-ounce cans kidney or pinto beans, rinsed and drained

One 15-ounce can diced tomatoes in juice, *not* drained

One 15-ounce can tomato sauce

2 tablespoons plus 1 teaspoon chili powder

1 teaspoon onion powder

1 teaspoon sugar

1 teaspoon ground cumin

1/2 teaspoon garlic powder

1/2 teaspoon dried oregano

1/4 teaspoon salt

One or two 12-ounce cans beef, drained and pulled into bite-sized pieces; or one or two 10-ounce cans chicken or turkey, rinsed, drained, and flaked

Black pepper (optional)

Combine all of the ingredients, then heat to the desired temperature. Add pepper to taste. (You may heat chili in the microwave or use a saucepan over the stove. Just be sure not to use an aluminum pan, as it can cause the tomatoes to take on an acidic taste.)

Serves 4

"Barbecued" Beef

This makes a great hot sandwich filling.

1 cup bottled barbecue sauce (or make
　　your own with the recipe below)

Two 12-ounce cans beef

4 French rolls (or hamburger buns in a
　　pinch), toasted

Combine the barbecue sauce with the beef and heat. Use as a filling for rolls to make sandwiches.

Serves 4

Homemade Barbecue Sauce

3/4 cup ketchup

3 tablespoons prepared mustard

1 tablespoon pancake syrup or
　　molasses

1 tablespoon brown sugar

1/2 teaspoon garlic powder

1/2 teaspoon onion powder

1/4 teaspoon salt

1/8 to 1/4 teaspoon cayenne

1/2 to 1 teaspoon Liquid Smoke®
　　(optional)

Combine all of the ingredients and stir until blended.

Makes about 1 cup

Corned Beef Burgers

One little 12-ounce can of corned beef makes about six burgers. They contain a good deal of protein, and the container hardly takes up any shelf space. Serve these burgers as you would regular hamburgers, with buns, ketchup, and pickles. Just be sure to buy corned beef, *not* corned beef hash.

One 12-ounce can corned beef	**¹/4 teaspoon ground black pepper**
1¹/2 teaspoons onion powder	**2 tablespoons butter, melted**
¹/2 teaspoon garlic powder	**¹/2 cup plain bread crumbs** (see Note)
¹/2 teaspoon paprika	**2 eggs**

Empty the corned beef into a medium-sized mixing bowl. Break it up and mix it together with your hands so that it's more like ground beef, rather than chunks. In a small bowl, whisk together the onion powder, garlic powder, paprika, and pepper. Sprinkle it all over the beef. Add the melted butter and mix, then add the bread crumbs and mix again. Lightly beat the two eggs, then combine them with the meat mixture. With your hands, make six patties from the mixture. You can cook these two ways:

Stovetop Method
Fry the patties with a little oil in a frying pan over medium heat. (Each side should take about 3 minutes in a hot skillet.) The patties are done when they are browned and heated through.

Oven Method

Preheat the oven to 375°F and prepare a cookie sheet with oil or nonstick spray. Dredge the patties in about ½ cup of plain bread crumbs, place them on your baking sheet, and bake for about 30 minutes, or until the patties are hot and starting to turn golden-brown.

Garnish as desired with ketchup, tomato, lettuce, and pickles.

Makes 6 patties

Note: Oven method requires an additional ½ cup plain bread crumbs.

Spicy Noodle, Cashew, and Beef Stir-Fry

I typically use chicken in dishes like this, but beef turns out to be a very good choice as well. If you can't find cans of stir-fry vegetables at your grocery store, don't worry. I'm giving you the separate equivalents, too.

8 ounces packaged thin noodles, such as spaghetti

1/4 cup cooking oil (preferably peanut or sesame)

1/4 teaspoon cayenne

1 cup cashews

Two 28-ounce cans stir-fry vegetables
or:
two 15-ounce cans bean sprouts, drained
two 8-ounce cans bamboo shoots, drained

one 8-ounce can sliced water chestnuts, drained

1/2 cup chopped roasted red peppers from a jar

one 15-ounce can small baby corn-on-the-cobs, drained

one 8-ounce can sliced carrots, drained

Two 12-ounce cans beef with gravy, drained and meat pulled apart into bite-sized chunks

3/4 cup teriyaki sauce

Cook the noodles according to the package directions, then drain.

Put the oil in a wok or frying pan over medium heat. Add the cayenne and cook for about 1 minute. Add the cashews and cook for another minute. Add the vegetables, stirring them so they're coated with oil, and cook them until they are hot. Stir in the noodles and beef and toss to coat. Add the teriyaki sauce, toss to coat, and continue to cook until the noodles are heated. Serve hot.

Serves 8

Beef Shepherd's Pie

Here's a fast and easy version of this perennial favorite. By the way, I don't salt the potatoes because the gravy is quite salty, but you may add salt if you like.

Two 15-ounce cans whole potatoes,
** *not* drained**
One 10.5-ounce can condensed
** cream of chicken soup, cream of**
** celery soup, or cream of**
** mushroom soup**
1/2 cup evaporated milk or whole
** milk**

Two 12-ounce cans beef in gravy
One 15-ounce can mixed vegetables,
** drained**
1 tablespoon butter
Extra butter or milk for topping
** (about 1 tablespoon)**

Preheat the oven to 400°F. Coat an 8 × 8-inch casserole dish with oil or nonstick spray.

Put the undrained potatoes in a medium saucepan, cover, and bring to a boil. Let the potatoes boil at least 5 minutes to soften them. They may boil longer while you prepare the rest of the dish.

In a medium-sized mixing bowl, combine the soup with the milk and whisk until smooth. Empty one can of beef with its gravy into the soup mixture. Drain the next can of beef, then empty the meat into the soup mixture. Add the mixed vegetables and stir to combine, then pour the beef mixture into the prepared baking dish.

Drain the potatoes and add the butter. Mash by hand or with a hand blender until smooth. If needed, add a little water or milk to smooth the potatoes. Carefully spoon the potatoes onto the meat mixture and spread over the top with a fork, forming a complete layer.

Brush the potato layer with a little melted butter or a little milk. Bake for 15 to 20 minutes, or until the top begins to brown.

Serves 4 to 6

Chicken and Potato Curry

This is about as easy a curry as curry gets, and it tastes great. It is best served over basmati rice, which has a slightly sweet fragrance and taste. Basmati rice can be found right next to the other rices in most grocery stores, but you may substitute any long-grain rice you have on hand.

1 cup basmati or other long-grain rice	1 cup sour cream
One 10-ounce can chicken, drained	2 teaspoons sugar
4 teaspoons curry powder	1/2 teaspoon onion powder
One 10.5-ounce can cream of chicken soup	1/2 teaspoon ground cinnamon
	One 15-ounce can whole white potatoes, drained

Prepare the rice according to the package directions.

Meanwhile, empty the chicken into a saucepan and sprinkle it with 1 teaspoon of the curry powder. Toss and flake to coat the chicken.

Stir in the soup and sour cream. Add the remaining 3 teaspoons of curry powder, the sugar, onion powder, and cinnamon, and stir well to combine. Put the saucepan on the stove over medium heat, stirring the chicken mixture often to keep it from burning.

Chop the potatoes into bite-sized chunks. Add them to the chicken mixture. Heat, stirring until everything is hot and completely blended. Serve hot over rice.

Serves 4

Chicken Croquettes

You can serve croquettes as you would crab cakes or use them as a substitute for a meat patty in a sandwich. If you serve them as they are, you may want to consider a sauce. Also note that you will have extra Spice Mix left over. This can be stored in a sealed jar for later use.

Spice Mix

1 tablespoon garlic powder

1 tablespoon onion powder

1 teaspoon ground black pepper

1 teaspoon paprika

1 teaspoon chili powder

1/4 teaspoon cayenne

1/4 teaspoon sugar

Croquettes

Two 10-ounce cans white chunk
   chicken, drained

2 tablespoons melted butter

1 tablespoon plus 1 teaspoon bottled
   lemon juice

1 cup plain bread crumbs, divided

2 teaspoons Spice Mix (above)

2 eggs

Preheat the oven to 375°F. Prepare a cookie sheet with oil or nonstick spray. In a small bowl or jar, combine the ingredients for the Spice Mix and blend well.

Rinse the chicken in a colander. Some chicken comes packed like tuna; other chicken comes in cubes. If it's like tuna, pull it apart with two forks. If it's in cubes, just work it between your fingers until it comes apart (which it does very easily).

Combine the melted butter, chicken, lemon juice, 1/2 cup of bread crumbs, and 2 teaspoons of Spice Mix. Lightly beat the eggs in a small bowl, then add to the chicken mixture. Blend well.

In another bowl, add 1 more teaspoon of Spice Mix to the remaining 1/2 cup of bread crumbs. With your hands, make a hamburger-sized patty from the chicken mixture, then coat it well in the bread-crumb mixture, and place it on the baking sheet. Repeat with the remaining chicken mixture. (You may have some bread crumbs left over.)

Bake for about 30 minutes, or until the croquettes are hot and starting to turn golden-brown.

Makes 6 croquettes

Creamed Chicken

Did your mom ever serve leftover meat and gravy over toast? This is a variation on that theme, but you can use toast, rice, or noodles. Also, you can cut calories by using low-fat milk and soup.

Rice, noodles, or toast for four

One 10-ounce can white chunk
   chicken, rinsed and drained

One 15-ounce can sliced potatoes,
   rinsed and drained

One 10.75-ounce can condensed
   cream of chicken soup

One 12-ounce can evaporated milk

2 tablespoons cornstarch dissolved
   in a little cold water

Salt and pepper

Prepare the rice or noodles according to the package directions. (If using toast, prepare it just before serving.)

Place the chicken in a medium saucepan. Dice the potatoes, then add them to the chicken. Add the soup, milk, and dissolved cornstarch, then stir over medium heat until boiling and thickened. Add salt and pepper as desired.

Serve over rice, noodles, or toast.

Serves 4

Southwestern Chicken Stew

You may want to serve this dish with warm tortillas or cornbread (page 145) on the side. You can find enchilada sauce in the grocery store in the Mexican food section, near the chilies and salsas, or you can make your own using the recipe found on page 252.

One 15-ounce can sliced potatoes

One 15-ounce can enchilada sauce or 2 cups homemade sauce (see page 252)

Two 10-ounce cans chicken, rinsed and drained

One 15-ounce can corn, drained, or hominy, rinsed and drained

1 cup chopped roasted red peppers from a jar

Chop or break the potatoes into bite-sized pieces. Put them in a saucepan with the enchilada sauce and cook over medium heat. Add the chicken, corn or hominy, and roasted red peppers. Heat to boiling, then lower the heat and simmer for 10 minutes. (You may simmer it longer, but give it at least 10 minutes to let the flavors steep.)

Serves 4

Chicken Parmesan

This one's very simple—great when you've had "one of those days."

8 ounces spaghetti
One 27-ounce jar of your favorite
spaghetti sauce (or see recipe on
page 247)

One or two 10-ounce cans chunk
white meat chicken, rinsed,
drained, and flaked
1 cup real shredded Parmesan cheese
(*not* the powdered kind)

Cook spaghetti according to package directions. Add chicken to sauce, then heat to boiling (you may use stovetop or microwave). Place cooked, drained spaghetti into a large serving bowl or pan (see Note). Pour heated sauce over spaghetti, then sprinkle cheese on top. Cheese should melt somewhat into the sauce, which is what you want.

If you wish the cheese to be completely melted, place dish in the microwave on high for 30 seconds or so. Or, you may place it in a hot oven (about 350°F) for about 10 minutes.

Serves 4

Note: Make sure you use microwave-safe or oven-safe dishes if you plan to melt cheese completely.

Chicken Pastitsio

Pastitsio is sort of a Greek version of lasagna, and though it's generally made with ground lamb, this recipe calls for chicken instead. As Americans, we're not accustomed to cinnamon in savory dishes. But it strikes a nice note here in contrast to the creamy cheese and meat.

8 ounces macaroni (about 2 cups)

One 12-ounce can evaporated milk
   or 1 3/4 cups whole milk

1 egg

1 cup shredded real Parmesan cheese
   (*not* the powdered kind)

One 10-ounce can white chunk
   chicken, rinsed and drained

1 teaspoon onion powder

1/2 teaspoon garlic powder

1/2 teaspoon dried oregano

Salt

One 8-ounce can tomato sauce

1/2 teaspoon ground cinnamon

1/4 teaspoon ground black pepper

1/8 teaspoon ground nutmeg

2 tablespoons cornstarch dissolved
   in a little cold water

2 tablespoons butter

Preheat the oven to 350°F. Lightly coat an 8 × 8-inch pan or dish with oil or nonstick spray. Prepare the macaroni according to the package directions. Drain and set aside.

In a medium-sized mixing bowl, combine 1/4 cup of the evaporated milk or whole milk with the egg. Stir in 1/3 cup of the Parmesan cheese, then add the cooked noodles to the mixture and toss to coat. Set aside.

In another medium-sized mixing bowl, season the chicken by combining it with the onion powder, garlic powder, oregano, and 1/4 teaspoon of salt. Toss to coat. Add the tomato sauce, cinnamon, pepper, 1/2 teaspoon of salt, and nutmeg, then toss together.

Place about half the pasta mixture in the 8 × 8-inch dish. Spread the chicken mixture on top of the pasta, then layer the remaining pasta over the chicken.

In a small or medium saucepan, combine the remaining 1 1/2 cups of milk, dissolved cornstarch, butter, and 1/2 teaspoon of salt. Stir over medium-high heat until the mixture begins to bubble. Add 1/3 cup of Parmesan cheese, and cook until the cheese has melted and the sauce has thickened. Pour the sauce over the pasta. Sprinkle the remaining 1/3 cup of Parmesan cheese over the top and bake for about 20 minutes, or until hot.

Serves 6

"Barbecued" Chicken

This makes great hot chicken sandwiches.

**1 cup bottled barbecue sauce (or make
your own using the recipe below)**

**Two or three 6.5-ounce cans chicken,
rinsed and drained**

**4 French rolls (or hamburger buns in a
pinch), toasted**

Combine the barbecue sauce with the chicken and heat. Use as a filling for rolls to make sandwiches.

Serves 4

Homemade Barbecue Sauce

3/4 cup ketchup

3 tablespoons prepared mustard

**1 tablespoon pancake syrup or
molasses**

1 tablespoon brown sugar

1/2 teaspoon garlic powder

1/2 teaspoon onion powder

1/4 teaspoon salt

1/8 to 1/4 teaspoon cayenne

**1/2 to 1 teaspoon Liquid Smoke®
(optional)**

Combine all of the ingredients and stir until blended.

Makes about 1 cup

Spicy Noodle, Cashew, and Chicken Stir-Fry

Make sure to use either the white chunk chicken or your favorite brand. I prefer the white to the mixed meats, and I also prefer to rinse the chicken first so that its taste is mild in this dish. If you can't find cans of stir-fried vegetables at your grocery store, don't worry: I'm giving you the separate equivalents, too.

8 ounces thin noodles, such as
  spaghetti
¹/₄ cup cooking oil (preferably peanut or
  sesame)
¹/₄ teaspoon cayenne
1 cup cashews
Two 28-ounce cans stir-fried
  vegetables *or:*
  two 15-ounce cans bean sprouts,
    drained
  two 8-ounce cans bamboo shoots,
    drained

one 8-ounce can sliced water
  chestnuts, drained
¹/₂ cup chopped roasted red
  peppers from a jar
one 15-ounce can small baby
  corn-on-the-cob, drained
one 8-ounce can sliced carrots,
  drained
Two or three 6-ounce cans white
  chunk chicken, rinsed and
  drained
³/₄ cup teriyaki sauce

Cook the noodles according to the package directions, then drain.

Put the oil in a wok or frying pan over medium heat. Add the cayenne and cook for about 1 minute. Add the cashews and cook for another minute. Add the vegetables, stirring them so they're coated with oil, and cook them until they are hot. Stir in the noodles and chicken, and toss to coat. Add the teriyaki sauce, toss to coat, and continue to cook until noodles are heated. Serve hot.

Serves 8

Mexican Chicken Bake

This dish couldn't be simpler, and it's packed with low-fat proteins. You can substitute pinto beans for either the black beans or the kidney beans, depending on what's in your pantry. And when it's time for leftovers, this casserole makes a great nacho topping or filling for enchiladas.

2 cups broken corn chips

1 teaspoon chili powder

1 tablespoon plus 1/2 teaspoon onion powder

1/2 teaspoon garlic powder

1/2 teaspoon ground cumin

1/2 teaspoon dried coriander

1/2 teaspoon ground black pepper

Two 10-ounce cans white chunk chicken, rinsed and drained

One 15-ounce can black beans, rinsed and drained

One 15-ounce can red kidney beans, rinsed and drained

One 15-ounce can corn, drained

One 4-ounce can diced chilies

One 2.25-ounce can sliced olives, drained

One 8-ounce can tomato sauce

1 cup prepared salsa

1 tablespoon dried cilantro

1/2 teaspoon salt

2 cups shredded Monterey Jack cheese

2 cups shredded Cheddar cheese

Sour cream, for garnish (optional)

Additional salsa for garnish (optional)

Preheat the oven to 350°F. Lightly coat a 9 × 13-inch baking dish with nonstick spray or cooking oil. Cover the bottom with the broken corn chips.

In a small bowl, blend together the chili powder, 1/2 teaspoon onion powder, garlic powder, cumin, coriander, and pepper with a fork. In a large mixing bowl, combine the chicken with the spice mixture. Add the beans, corn, chilies, olives, tomato sauce, and salsa. Mix well, then add the cilantro, 1 tablespoon onion powder, and salt, and mix well again.

Spread half the chicken mixture over the corn chips in the dish. Cover with 1 cup each of Jack and Cheddar cheese. Spread the remaining chicken mixture over the cheese layer, then cover with the remaining cheese. Bake for 25 to 30 minutes, or until the cheese is thoroughly melted. Garnish with sour cream and salsa if desired.

Serves 8

Chicken Shepherd's Pie

This is something very easy to make after work or anytime you want comfort food. If you have 2 cups of leftover mashed potatoes, you may substitute them for the potatoes called for in this recipe.

Two 15-ounce cans whole potatoes

One 10.5-ounce can condensed cream of chicken soup, cream of celery soup, or cream of mushroom soup

1/2 cup evaporated milk or whole milk

Three 6-ounce cans chicken, drained

One 15-ounce can mixed vegetables, drained

1 tablespoon butter

Extra butter or milk for topping (about 1 tablespoon)

Preheat the oven to 400°F. Coat an 8 × 8-inch casserole dish with oil or nonstick spray.

Put the undrained potatoes in a medium saucepan, cover, and bring to a boil. Let the potatoes boil for at least 5 minutes to soften them. They may boil longer while you prepare the rest of the dish.

In a medium-sized mixing bowl, combine the soup with the milk and whisk until smooth. Add the chicken and mixed vegetables, stirring to combine. Pour the mixture into the prepared baking dish.

Drain the potatoes and add the butter. Mash by hand or with a hand blender until smooth.

If needed, add a little water or milk to smooth the potatoes. Carefully spoon the potatoes over the chicken mixture and spread over the top with a fork, forming a complete layer.

Brush the potato layer with a little melted butter or a little milk. Bake for 15 to 20 minutes, or until the top begins to brown.

Serves 4 to 6

Chicken Pot Pie

Chicken pot pie is perhaps the original comfort food. This version is super easy and a deliciously warm treat on a cold night. To trim calories or salt, try low-fat and low-sodium soup.

Two pie crust pastries
One or two 10-ounce cans chicken,
    drained
Two 15-ounce cans mixed vegetables,
    drained, or one can mixed
    vegetables, drained, and one can
    sliced potatoes, rinsed, drained,
    and chopped

One 10.75-ounce can cream of
    chicken soup, cream of
    mushroom soup, or cream of
    celery soup

Preheat oven to 425°F. Thaw pie crusts as package directs. Lightly coat a 9-inch pie pan with oil or nonstick spray. In a medium mixing bowl, combine chicken, vegetables, and soup. Line pie pan with one pie crust. Pour chicken mixture into the lined pie pan and smooth over. Top with second crust, crimping edges together. Cut slits in the top pie crust.

Bake 30 minutes, or until crust turns golden brown.

Serves 4 to 6

Pineapple-Ham Rice

Tell the kids it's Hawaiian night and relax. Consider serving Coconut Custard (page 282) for dessert.

Some teriyaki sauces are too mild, so I suggest teriyaki *marinade* instead. If all you've got is a mild sauce, spice it up with some extra ground ginger (about ½ teaspoon).

One 15-ounce can chicken broth
    plus ¼ cup water or 1 teaspoon/
    cube chicken bouillon plus 2 cups
    water (see Note)
1 cup long-grain rice
Two 5-ounce cans ham, drained
Cooking oil for sautéing

One 20-ounce can crushed
    pineapple, juice reserved
¼ cup teriyaki marinade
3 tablespoons brown sugar
3 tablespoons cornstarch dissolved
    in a little cold water

Put the chicken broth or bouillon and water in a medium saucepan and bring to a boil. Add the rice and cook according to the package directions.

Meanwhile, dice the ham. Sauté it in a frying pan with a little cooking oil until it starts to brown.

Add enough water to the reserved pineapple juice to make 1 cup. In a medium-sized saucepan, combine the pineapple, pineapple juice and water, teriyaki marinade, brown sugar, and the cornstarch mixture, and bring to a boil. Cook for another couple of minutes, until the sauce thickens. Add the browned diced ham and serve over rice.

Serves 4

Note: If you're using instant rice, simply replace the water called for in the package directions with an equal amount of chicken broth.

Penne with Ham, Tomato, and Olives

When you want something very easy but full of taste, this one's a good choice. Makes a great fast dinner or lunch.

8 ounces penne pasta

One 28-ounce can crushed tomatoes

One tablespoon olive oil

2 teaspoons dried basil

2 teaspoons garlic powder

1 teaspoon sugar

1/2 teaspoon salt

1/4 teaspoon ground black pepper

One 2.25-ounce can sliced black olives, drained

Two 5-ounce cans ham, drained and chopped

Real grated Parmesan cheese as garnish (optional)

Cook pasta according to package directions. In a medium saucepan, heat tomatoes, oil, basil, garlic powder, sugar, salt, and pepper until boiling. Toss sauce with drained pasta. Add olives and ham and toss again to coat. Garnish with Parmesan cheese at serving time, if desired.

Serves 4

Creamy Hominy with Ham

This is a one-saucepan meal, terrific comfort food for winter or a great way not to use the oven if you don't want to heat up your house in the summer.

One 12-ounce can evaporated milk
One 10.75-ounce can condensed cream of celery soup or cream of chicken soup
Two 5-ounce cans ham, *not* drained
1/2 cup shredded Cheddar cheese

2 tablespoons cornstarch dissolved in a little cold water
Two 15-ounce cans hominy, drained
One 2.25-ounce can sliced black olives, not drained

Stir the milk and soup together in a medium-sized saucepan over medium heat. Add the liquid from the ham cans, then dice the ham. When the soup has blended with the milk, add the cheese. Stir frequently to prevent burning. When the cheese has melted, make sure the soup mixture is nearly boiling (there will be little bubbles around the edges of the pan) and add the cornstarch mixture. Cook for another minute or so, until thickened, then add the ham, hominy, and olives. Heat for a minute or two, just to bring the hominy up to temperature.

Serves 6

Turkey Shepherd's Pie

Easy as pie . . .

Two 15-ounce cans whole potatoes, *not* drained

One 10.5-ounce can condensed cream of chicken, cream of celery, or cream of mushroom soup

1/2 cup evaporated milk or whole milk

Three 6-ounce cans turkey

One 15-ounce can mixed vegetables, drained

1 tablespoon butter

Extra butter or milk for topping (about 1 tablespoon)

Preheat the oven to 400°F. Coat an 8 × 8-inch casserole dish with oil or nonstick spray.

Put the undrained potatoes in a medium saucepan, cover, and bring to a boil. Let the potatoes boil at least 5 minutes to soften them. If you wish, you may boil them longer while you prepare the rest of the dish.

In a medium-sized mixing bowl, combine the soup with the milk and whisk until smooth. Add the turkey and mixed vegetables, stirring to combine. Pour the mixture into the prepared baking dish.

Drain the potatoes and add the butter. Mash by hand or with a hand blender until smooth. If needed, add a little water or milk to smooth the potatoes. Carefully spoon the potatoes over the turkey mixture and spread them over the top with a fork, forming a complete layer.

Brush the potato layer with a little melted butter or a little milk. Bake for 15 to 20 minutes, or until the top begins to brown.

Serves 4 to 6

Curried Turkey and Rice Bake

This is a one-dish meal (my favorite kind!). It's perfect for a cold winter evening when you're craving a little comfort food but still want something a bit different.

One 10.75-ounce can condensed
   cream of mushroom soup

¹/₂ cup sour cream

1 tablespoon sugar

2 teaspoons curry powder

¹/₂ teaspoon ground cinnamon

¹/₂ teaspoon onion powder

¹/₂ teaspoon ground cumin

1 cup basmati or long-grain white
   rice

One 10-ounce can turkey, drained

¹/₃ cup golden raisins (black raisins are
   okay, too)

¹/₃ cup broken or chopped cashews
   (or almonds)

Preheat the oven to 350°F. Combine the soup, 1 cup of water, and the sour cream in an 8 × 8-inch baking dish, stirring until well blended. Next add the sugar, curry, cinnamon, onion powder, and cumin. Stir well. Add the rice, turkey, raisins, and nuts, blending well. Cover (if you don't have a cover for your dish, simply use aluminum foil). Bake for about 45 minutes, or until rice is cooked.

Serves 4

Curried Chicken and Rice Bake

Follow recipe for Curried Turkey and Rice Bake above, and substitute one 10-ounce can of chicken for the turkey.

Southwestern Turkey Stew

You may want to serve this dish with warm tortillas on the side. You can find enchilada sauce in the grocery store in the Mexican food section, near the chilies and salsas, or you may make your own using the recipe on page 252.

One 15-ounce can sliced potatoes,   **One 15-ounce can corn, drained, or**
    rinsed and drained   **hominy, rinsed and drained**
One 15-ounce can enchilada sauce   **1 cup chopped roasted red peppers**
    or 2 cups homemade sauce   **from a jar**
Two 10-ounce cans turkey, rinsed
    and drained

Chop or break the potatoes into bite-sized pieces. Put the potatoes in a saucepan with the enchilada sauce over medium heat. Add the turkey, corn or hominy, and roasted red peppers. Heat to boiling, then lower the heat and simmer for 10 minutes. (You may simmer it longer, but give it at least ten minutes to let the flavors steep.)

Serves 4

Fish and Seafood

CHAPTER 6

Easy Seafood Lasagna

I tried to make this without boiling the noodles first, but the time required in the oven to soften them ends up drying out the filling. So, this lasagna requires that you boil the noodles first. It's quite a simple dish nevertheless and has a relatively short baking time, since the noodles are precooked (like everything else). With this recipe, you may use just about any type of mild seafood you like—substitute tuna or use all crab or all shrimp.

16 ounces uncooked lasagna noodles   **Quick Seafood Sauce (page 243)**

Filling:

One 32-ounce container ricotta cheese

1/2 cup real grated Parmesan or Romano cheese (not the powdered kind)

2 eggs, lightly beaten

1 teaspoon garlic powder

1 teaspoon dried basil

1/8 teaspoon salt

2 cups shredded mozzarella or Jack cheese

Preheat the oven to 350°F. Lightly coat a 9 × 13-inch pan with nonstick spray or cooking oil. Prepare the lasagna noodles according to the package directions. Meanwhile, prepare the

Quick Seafood Sauce and set it aside. In a medium- to large-sized mixing bowl, combine the ricotta cheese, grated Parmesan or Romano, eggs, garlic, basil, and salt. Stir until smooth.

When the noodles have been cooked and drained, carefully lay about four noodles in your 9 × 13-inch pan, the goal being to cover the bottom in one layer. Ladle 1½ cups of Seafood Sauce over the noodles and spread evenly. Spoon about half of the ricotta mixture onto the sauce, and gently smooth it out. (It doesn't have to be perfect—the heat will cause the cheese to melt and spread itself evenly.) Sprinkle ½ cup of mozzarella or Jack cheese on top of the ricotta mixture. Lay another four or so noodles on top of the cheese layer. Top that with 1½ cups of sauce, the remaining ricotta, then another ½ cup shredded mozzarella or Jack cheese.

Place the remaining four noodles on top of last layer as before, then pour the remaining sauce (about 2 cups) on top, spreading it evenly.

Cover the lasagna with foil and bake for 35 minutes. Remove the lasagna from the oven and take off the foil. Sprinkle with the remaining cup of shredded cheese and bake, uncovered, for 10 more minutes, until the cheese on top is nice and bubbly. Let the lasagna stand for about 10 minutes before serving so that the cheese is not dangerously hot.

Serves 8

Seafood Curry

This is an easy dish, but please note that crab and shrimp are mild-tasting, and the curry can overpower them a bit if you don't season carefully.

1 cup rice
One 10.75-ounce can condensed
    cream of mushroom soup
1 cup sour cream or yogurt
2 to 3 teaspoons curry powder
    (depending on your brand and taste)
2 teaspoons sugar

1/2 teaspoon onion powder
1/2 teaspoon ground cinnamon
Two 6-ounce cans crab or one
    6-ounce can crab and one
    6-ounce can tiny shrimp, drained,
    with crab cartilage removed if
    necessary

Prepare the rice according to the package directions.

Combine the soup, sour cream or yogurt, curry powder, sugar, onion powder, cinnamon, and seafood in a medium-sized saucepan. Mix well, and cook over medium heat until hot and bubbly. Serve over rice.

Serves 4

Pasta with Lemon, Basil, and Clams

The lemon in this recipe makes a nice backdrop for the basil and clams. Consider serving this dish with some lightly toasted sourdough bread and butter and your favorite white wine.

8 ounces pasta such as linguine,
    spaghetti, or fettuccine
2 tablespoons butter
1/4 cup olive oil
1/4 cup bottled lemon juice
1 teaspoon dried basil

1/2 teaspoon garlic powder
1/2 teaspoon salt
1/2 teaspoon onion powder
1/4 teaspoon dried oregano
Two 6-ounce cans chopped clams,
    not drained

Cook the pasta according to the package directions.

Meanwhile, melt the butter in a medium saucepan. Add the oil, lemon juice, basil, garlic powder, salt, onion powder, and oregano. Stir until blended and heated. If the noodles are not ready, simply cover the lemon-basil mixture and let it simmer on very low heat. Just before serving, add both cans of clams with their juice to the lemon-basil mixture, and continue to heat just to bring up the temperature again.

Drain the pasta, then pour the lemon-basil mixture over it and toss to coat. Serve at once.

Serves 4

Clam Chowder Pie

I love clam chowder, and this "pie" makes a great alternative. It feels more like a meal.

One 9-inch pie-crust pastry

One 15-ounce can sliced potatoes, rinsed and drained

3/4 cup evaporated milk or whole milk

Two 6-ounce cans clams, drained, liquid reserved

1 1/2 teaspoons onion powder

1/2 teaspoon celery salt

1/4 teaspoon ground black pepper

1/4 teaspoon garlic powder

1/4 teaspoon Worcestershire sauce

1 tablespoon butter

1 tablespoon cornstarch, dissolved in a little cold water

Preheat the oven to 425°F. Prepare the pie crust according to the package directions. Coat a 9-inch pie pan with a little oil or nonstick spray.

Dice the potatoes and set aside. In a medium saucepan, combine the milk and 1/2 cup of liquid reserved from the clams. Add the onion powder, celery salt, black pepper, garlic powder, and Worcestershire sauce. Stir until dissolved, then add the butter and dissolved cornstarch. Heat over medium-high heat until bubbly and thickened (about 5 minutes).

When the sauce has thickened, add the potatoes and clams and stir to combine. Pour the clam mixture into the prepared pie plate. Place the pie crust over the top, crimping it down along the circumference of the pan and tearing away any extra. Make four small slits in the crust. Bake for 25 to 30 minutes, or until the crust is golden-brown.

Serves 6

Note: To keep the pastry edges from burning, wrap a little aluminum foil around the outside of the pie. An easy way to do this is to place a whole sheet of foil over the pie, crimp it down around the edges, then carefully cut out a large hole in the middle. Remove the foil about halfway through the baking process.

Crab Tostadas with Cumin-Lime-Mint Dressing

This is a very light dish, perfect for a summer lunch or dinner. It's also low in fat, since there's no oil in the dressing. I like a mild crab flavor, but if you prefer a stronger taste, don't drain the crab before you place it on the tortilla. I also advise that you use very little, if any, salsa. It can really overpower the crab. I suggest making the dressing first so that the mint has a chance to steep.

Cumin-Lime-Mint Dressing

1/3 cup bottled lime juice

1 tablespoon dried mint

1 tablespoon sugar

2 tablespoons water

1/2 teaspoon ground cumin

1/8 teaspoon salt

Tostadas

3 crisp tostada shells (about 6 inches in diameter)

One 6-ounce can crab

Torn or shredded iceberg lettuce for three

Sour cream, salsa, sliced olives, or shredded Cheddar for garnish (optional)

Combine the dressing ingredients and shake or blend well. Set aside for a few minutes.

Prepare the tostada shells according to the package directions.

Place one-third of the crab on each of the three tostadas. Place small mounds of lettuce on top of the crab. Drizzle approximately 2 tablespoons of dressing on each. Garnish with a small dollop of sour cream, salsa, Cheddar, or olives, if desired.

Serves 3

Crab Divan

Here's another quick and tasty way to prepare crab. Serve this dish plain or on a bed of rice.

One 15-ounce can asparagus spears
    and tips, drained
One 10.75-ounce can condensed
    cream of chicken soup
1 cup sour cream
Two 6-ounce cans crab, drained

1/2 cup shredded Parmesan cheese or
    Swiss cheese (or four Swiss cheese
    slices)
2 teaspoons bread crumbs (optional)
Butter (optional)

Preheat the oven to 350°F. Coat an 8 × 8-inch casserole dish with oil or nonstick spray.

Empty the asparagus into the prepared baking dish. In a medium-sized mixing bowl, combine the soup and sour cream, stirring until well combined. Gently stir in the crab. Pour the crab mixture over the asparagus. Sprinkle the crab mixture with cheese or top with cheese slices. If desired, sprinkle the cheese with bread crumbs and dot with butter.

Bake for about 15 minutes, or until the cheese is bubbly.

Serves 4

Crab Newburg

This dish may seem a little decadent, but you can trim calories by using nonfat evaporated milk. Aside from the egg yolks, however, the ingredients are not too rich. Serve over toast points or rice. If you like a stronger crab flavor, don't drain the crab before using it.

One 12-ounce can evaporated milk

1 tablespoon cornstarch

2 egg yolks

2 tablespoons sherry or white wine

1/2 teaspoon salt

1/2 teaspoon ground nutmeg

Pinch cayenne

1 tablespoon butter

Two 6-ounce cans crab, drained, cartilage removed

Toast points or rice for serving (enough for four; see Note)

Pinch dried parsley or chives for garnish (optional)

In a medium saucepan, whisk or beat the milk and cornstarch until the cornstarch has dissolved. Add the egg yolks and beat with an electric beater or hand blender, or simply whisk repeatedly until smooth. Add the sherry or wine, salt, nutmeg, cayenne, and butter. Place the mixture on the stove over medium heat and bring to a boil. Stir until the butter has melted and the sauce has thickened.

Stir in the crab while the sauce is still at a boil and remove from the heat. Serve immediately over toast points or rice and garnish with parsley or chives, if desired.

Serves 4

Note: Toast points are simply slices of toast with the crusts removed, sliced diagonally.

Salmon Shepherd's Pie

Salmon contains high levels of omega-3 fatty acids, something many of us don't get enough of. This recipe is quite easy, and if you have leftover mashed potatoes, you can easily substitute them for the potatoes called for in this dish. (You'll need about 2 cups.)

**Two 15-ounce cans whole potatoes,
  not drained**

**One 10.5-ounce can condensed
  cream of chicken, cream of
  celery, or cream of mushroom
  soup**

**1/2 cup evaporated milk or whole
  milk**

**One 15-ounce can salmon, drained,
  bone and cartilage removed if
  desired**

**One 15-ounce can mixed vegetables,
  drained**

1 tablespoon butter

**Extra butter or milk for topping
  (about 1 tablespoon)**

Preheat the oven to 400°F. Coat an 8 × 8-inch casserole dish with oil or nonstick spray.

Put the undrained potatoes in a medium saucepan, cover, and bring to a boil. Let the potatoes boil for at least 5 minutes to soften them. They may boil longer while you prepare the rest of the dish.

In a medium-sized mixing bowl, combine the soup with the milk and whisk until smooth. Add the salmon and mixed vegetables, stirring to combine. Pour the mixture into the prepared baking dish.

Drain the potatoes and add the butter. Mash by hand or with a hand blender until smooth. If needed, add a little water or milk to smooth the potatoes. Carefully spoon the potatoes over the salmon mixture and spread with a fork, forming a complete layer.

Brush the potato layer with a little melted butter or a little milk. Bake for 15 to 20 minutes, or until the top begins to brown.

Serves 4 to 6

Salmon Tetrazzini

In many cases, canned salmon is less expensive than tuna, making it a cost-effective source of protein. It's not necessary to remove all the skin and bones, as they are an excellent source of calcium and quite soft. I always remove them for aesthetic reasons, but it's your call.

8 ounces spaghetti, linguine, or
   spaghettini

One 15-ounce can salmon, drained

One 12-ounce can evaporated milk

One 10.75-ounce can condensed
   cream of mushroom soup

One 7-ounce can sliced mushrooms,
   not drained

1/4 cup dry white wine or sherry
   (optional)

1 tablespoon onion powder

1/2 teaspoon garlic powder

1/8 teaspoon ground black pepper

1/8 teaspoon salt (optional)

1/2 cup real shredded Parmesan
   cheese (*not* the powdered kind)

1/4 cup bread crumbs

Cook the pasta according to the package directions. Lightly coat a 9 × 13-inch baking dish or pan with cooking oil or nonstick spray. Drain the pasta, then spread it in the bottom of the baking dish.

Preheat the oven to 375°F.

Remove the skin and bones (if desired) from the salmon, then place it in a medium saucepan.

Add the milk, soup, mushrooms *with liquid*, wine or sherry, onion powder, garlic powder, black pepper, salt if desired, and ¼ cup of Parmesan cheese. Cook over medium heat until everything is blended, the cheese has melted, and the mixture begins to boil.

Pour the mixture evenly over the noodles in the baking dish. Mix the bread crumbs with the remaining Parmesan cheese, then sprinkle over the top.

Bake for 25 to 30 minutes. When it's ready, the top should be crisp, with bubbling and browning around the edges.

Serves 4 to 6

VARIATION

Tuna Tetrazzini

Follow the directions above, substituting two or three 6-ounce cans of tuna, drained and flaked, for the salmon.

Baked Salmon Croquettes

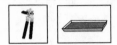

Here's another great way to use canned salmon, an excellent source of calcium and protein. Try serving these with Lemon-Horseradish Sauce (page 240).

Spice Mix

1 teaspoon garlic powder

1 teaspoon onion powder

1/2 teaspoon ground black pepper

1/2 teaspoon paprika

1/2 teaspoon chili powder

1/4 teaspoon cayenne

1/4 teaspoon salt

1/4 teaspoon sugar

One 16-ounce can salmon

2 tablespoons melted butter

1 tablespoon bottled lemon juice

3/4 cup plain bread crumbs, divided

2 eggs

Preheat the oven to 375°F. Lightly coat a baking sheet with cooking oil or nonstick spray.

Combine the ingredients for the spice mix and set aside. Drain the salmon. You may use the salmon as it is, or you may pick out the bones and skin (which provide much calcium).

In a medium-sized mixing bowl, combine the salmon, butter, lemon juice, half the bread crumbs, and 1½ teaspoons of the Spice Mix. Lightly beat the eggs, then combine them with the salmon mixture.

Put the remaining bread crumbs in a bowl and mix with 1 teaspoon of Spice Mix (you'll have a little Spice Mix left over). With your hands, make six patties out of the salmon mixture. Dredge (coat) each in bread crumbs, and place on a baking sheet. Bake for about 30 minutes, until the croquettes are hot and golden-brown.

Makes 6 croquettes

Shrimp-Noodle Bake

This dish has a few steps but they're all very easy. And the coral color of the shrimp looks really nice in the noodles.

6 ounces wide egg noodles

One 12-ounce can evaporated milk

1/4 cup cornstarch dissolved in a
   little cold water

2 tablespoons butter

3/4 teaspoon salt

3/4 teaspoon dried dill

1/2 cup real shredded Parmesan
   cheese (*not* the powdered kind)

One 6-ounce can tiny or medium
   shrimp, drained

One 3-ounce can dried French
   onions (optional; see Note)

Preheat the oven to 350°F. Coat an 8 × 8-inch baking dish with a little oil or nonstick spray. Cook the noodles according to the package directions.

In a medium saucepan, combine the milk, 1 1/2 cups of water, dissolved cornstarch, butter, salt, and dill. Cook over medium-high heat, stirring often. When the mixture begins to bubble and thicken, add the Parmesan cheese and stir, cooking until the cheese has melted and the sauce has thickened. Remove from the heat.

Add the shrimp and cooked noodles and stir. Pour the mixture into the prepared baking dish.

Bake for 25 minutes, then garnish the top with dried onion rings, if desired, and bake 2 minutes more, or until hot.

Serves 6

Note: Some noodles will float to the top during cooking and become a little crispy. The dried French onions help minimize that.

Penne with Pesto, Tuna, and Olives

This one's simple and full of flavor. It's also easily doubled if you've got a big family or just want extra for leftovers.

8 ounces penne or other tubular pasta
Two 6-ounce cans tuna, drained
One 8- to 10-ounce jar pesto sauce
One 2.25-ounce can sliced black olives, drained

Real grated Parmesan cheese for garnish (not the powdered kind; optional)

Prepare the pasta according to the package directions. Drain the noodles. While they're still hot, toss them together with the tuna, pesto sauce, and olives in a medium-sized mixing bowl or pasta bowl. Sprinkle with Parmesan cheese if desired. Serve immediately.

Serves 4

Tuna Shepherd's Pie

If you have leftover mashed potatoes, you can easily substitute them for the potatoes called for in this dish. (You'll need about 2 cups.) This is a very easy twist on traditional shepherd's pie.

Two 15-ounce cans whole potatoes, *not* **drained**
One 10.5-ounce can condensed cream of chicken, cream of celery, or cream of mushroom soup
1/2 cup evaporated milk or whole milk

Three 6-ounce cans tuna, drained
One 15-ounce can mixed vegetables, drained
1 tablespoon butter
Extra butter or milk for topping
(about 1 tablespoon)

Preheat the oven to 400°F. Coat an 8 × 8-inch casserole dish with oil or nonstick spray.

Put the undrained potatoes in a medium saucepan, cover, and bring to a boil. Let the potatoes boil at least 5 minutes to soften them. They may boil longer while you prepare the rest of the dish.

In a medium-sized mixing bowl, combine the soup with the milk and whisk until smooth. Add the tuna and mixed vegetables, stirring to combine. Pour the mixture into the prepared baking dish.

Drain the potatoes and add the butter. Mash by hand or with a hand blender until smooth. If needed, add a little water or milk to smooth the potatoes. Carefully spoon the potatoes over the tuna mixture and spread over the top with a fork, forming a complete layer.

Brush the potato layer with a little melted butter or a little milk. Bake for 15 to 20 minutes, or until the top begins to brown.

Serves 4 to 6

Spicy Noodle, Cashew, and Tuna Stir-Fry

If you don't find canned stir-fried vegetables at your store, don't worry: I'm giving you the equivalents here to make your own.

8 ounces thin noodles, such as
  spaghetti

1/4 cup cooking oil (preferably peanut or
  sesame)

1/4 teaspoon cayenne

1 cup cashews

Two 28-ounce cans stir-fried
  vegetables *or*:

  two 15-ounce cans bean sprouts,
    drained

  two 8-ounce cans bamboo shoots,
    drained

one 8-ounce can sliced water
  chestnuts, drained

1/2 cup chopped roasted red
  pepper from a jar

one 15-ounce can small baby
  corn-on-the-cob, drained

one 8-ounce can sliced carrots,
  drained

Two or three 6-ounce cans white
  chunk tuna, rinsed and drained

3/4 cup teriyaki sauce

Cook the noodles according to the package directions, then drain.

Put the oil in wok or frying pan over medium heat. Add the cayenne and cook for about 1 minute. Add the cashews and cook for another minute. Add the vegetables, stirring them so they're coated with oil, and cook until they are hot. Stir in the noodles and tuna, and toss to coat. Add the teriyaki sauce, toss to coat, and continue to cook until noodles are heated. Serve hot.

Serves 8

Tuna-Potato Bake

Ah, tuna. It's like the Old Faithful of the fish world. This dish provides ample amounts of protein through the tuna, the eggs, and the cheese (plus some in the milk). It's very hearty and a breeze to make. Good for a cold winter evening, too.

Two 15-ounce cans sliced potatoes, rinsed and drained

One 12-ounce can evaporated milk (nonfat is okay)

One 10.75-ounce can condensed cream of celery soup

4 eggs

1 teaspoon onion powder

1/4 teaspoon salt

1/4 teaspoon ground black pepper

Two 6-ounce cans tuna, drained

1 1/2 cups shredded cheese (Cheddar, American, Swiss, or Parmesan)

Preheat the oven to 350°F. Coat an 8 × 8-inch pan with oil or nonstick spray.

Dice the potatoes and put them aside. In a medium mixing bowl, whisk together the milk, celery soup, eggs, onion powder, salt, and pepper until smooth. (You might have tiny pieces of soup that are not completely absorbed; that's okay because they'll dissolve in the heat.) Stir in the tuna, cheese, and diced potatoes, then pour the mixture into the prepared pan. It should come nearly to the top (if you're using at least a 2-inch-high dish).

Bake for 55 to 60 minutes, or until a knife inserted into the center comes out clean. The edges should be golden-brown.

Serves 6

"Barbecued" Tuna

This makes great tuna sandwiches.

1 cup of your favorite barbecue sauce
(or make your own with the recipe below)

Two or three 6-ounce cans tuna,
rinsed and drained

4 French rolls (or hamburger buns in a
pinch), **toasted**

Combine the barbecue sauce with the tuna and heat until boiling. Use as a filling for rolls to make sandwiches.

Serves 4

Homemade Barbecue Sauce

3/4 cup ketchup
3 tablespoons prepared mustard
1 tablespoon pancake syrup or
    molasses
1 tablespoon brown sugar

1/2 teaspoon garlic powder
1/2 teaspoon onion powder
1/4 teaspoon salt
1/8 to 1/4 teaspoon cayenne
1/2 to 1 teaspoon Liquid Smoke®
    (optional)

Combine all of the ingredients and stir until blended.

Makes about 1 cup.

Breads and Pastries

CHAPTER 7

Applesauce-Raisin Bread

Apples are probably my favorite fruit, and I don't think I know anyone who doesn't have some applesauce somewhere in the pantry. This is an easy, tasty spice bread just perfect for kids or to serve to guests with a steaming mug of tea.

1 3/4 cups all-purpose flour
1/2 teaspoon baking soda
1/2 teaspoon salt
2 teaspoons baking powder
1 teaspoon ground cinnamon
1/2 teaspoon ground nutmeg
1/2 teaspoon ground cloves
1/2 teaspoon ground ginger

1 egg
1/3 cup cooking oil
1 teaspoon vanilla extract
1 cup sugar
1 cup applesauce
1/2 cup currants or raisins
1/2 cup chopped nuts (optional)

Preheat the oven to 350°F. Lightly coat a 9 × 5-inch loaf pan with oil or nonstick spray.

In a medium mixing bowl, combine the flour, baking soda, salt, baking powder, cinnamon, nutmeg, cloves, and ginger. Stir with a fork to sift and blend.

In another medium mixing bowl, lightly beat the egg, then add the oil, vanilla, and sugar. Beat until smooth. Alternately add batches of flour mixture and applesauce to the egg-and-sugar mixture until all are combined and beaten smooth. Stir in the currants or raisins, and nuts if desired. Pour into the prepared pan and bake for about 50 minutes, or until a knife inserted into the center comes out clean. Cool for 10 minutes, then wrap in plastic for easier slicing.

Makes 1 loaf (eighteen 1/2-inch slices)

Cherry-Walnut Bread

Fruit breads are very easy to whip up, and they make great snacks or school-lunch additions. This one also makes for nice quiet time with a steaming cup of Earl Grey tea. Think about serving it during the holidays.

2 cups all-purpose flour

1 teaspoon ground cinnamon

1/2 teaspoon ground nutmeg

1/2 teaspoon baking soda

1/2 teaspoon salt

2 teaspoons baking powder

1 cup sugar

1/4 cup cooking oil

1 egg

1 teaspoon vanilla extract

One 15-ounce can tart pitted
   cherries, drained

1/2 cup chopped walnuts

Preheat the oven to 350°F. Coat a 9 × 5-inch loaf pan with oil or nonstick spray.

In a medium-sized mixing bowl, combine the flour, cinnamon, nutmeg, baking soda, salt, and baking powder, using a fork to stir and distribute.

In another bowl, combine the sugar, oil, egg, and vanilla, beating until smooth. Add the cherries and continue to beat for another minute or so. You should beat until you have smaller pieces of cherry, but not until smooth. Add the flour mixture, beating or stirring until completely moistened. Stir in the walnuts.

Pour into the prepared pan and bake for 50 to 55 minutes, or until a knife inserted into the center of the bread comes out clean. Let stand for 10 minutes to cool. For easier slicing, wrap the loaf in plastic wrap.

Makes 1 loaf (eighteen ½-inch slices)

Cornbread

Cornbread is a great side with chili (page 80) or nearly any Southern-style or Southwestern food. And it's really easy to make.

1¹/2 cups all-purpose flour

1¹/2 cups cornmeal

¹/2 cup sugar

2 tablespoons baking powder

1¹/2 teaspoons salt

2 eggs

One 12-ounce can evaporated milk
    or 1¹/2 cups whole milk

¹/3 cup cooking oil

One 15-ounce can corn, drained

Preheat the oven to 425°F. Coat a 9 × 13-inch pan with oil or nonstick spray.

In a medium-sized mixing bowl, combine the flour, cornmeal, sugar, baking powder, and salt, and stir well with a fork or whisk.

In a small bowl, *lightly* beat the eggs. Add the milk, cooking oil, and then the eggs to the flour mixture and stir just until moistened and combined (don't overbeat). Stir in the corn, then pour the batter into the prepared pan and bake for 15 to 18 minutes, or until a knife inserted into the center comes out clean.

Serves 8

Green-Chili Cornbread

Follow the recipe above, adding one 4-ounce can of diced chilies, drained, to the batter.

Lemon Bread

This bread is terrific for afternoon tea or in a sack lunch.

1³/4 cups all purpose flour
1/2 teaspoon baking soda
1/2 teaspoon salt
2 teaspoons baking powder
1 cup sugar
1/3 cup cooking oil

2 eggs
1/3 cup bottled lemon juice
1 teaspoon vanilla extract
1/4 cup evaporated milk or whole milk

Preheat the oven to 350°F. Coat a 9 × 5-inch loaf pan with oil or nonstick spray.

In a medium-sized mixing bowl, using a fork, combine the flour, baking soda, salt, and baking powder. In another bowl, combine the sugar, oil, eggs, lemon juice, vanilla, and milk. Stir or beat into the flour mixture until smooth. Pour the batter into the prepared pan and bake for 50 to 55 minutes, or until a knife inserted into the center comes out clean.

Makes 1 loaf (eighteen 1/2-inch slices)

Lemon–Poppy Seed Bread

Follow the directions above, adding 1 tablespoon of poppy seeds to the batter.

Lemon-Raisin Bread

Follow the directions for Lemon Bread, above, and add 1 cup of raisins or currants to the batter.

Molasses Wheat Bread

Here's an easy way to bake bread (no yeast!) and a delicious way to enrich your diet with iron, something many of us are a little short on. This bread tastes a lot like Boston brown bread, but you don't need to steam it. You can buy whole-wheat flour at most grocery stores these days.

1 cup white all-purpose flour

2 cups whole-wheat flour

1/2 cup sugar

1 teaspoon salt

1 teaspoon baking soda

One 12-ounce can evaporated milk

1/2 cup molasses

1 cup raisins, currants, dried
    cranberries, or chopped dates
    (optional)

Preheat the oven to 325°F. Coat a 9 × 5-inch loaf pan with oil or nonstick spray.

In a medium or large mixing bowl, combine the flours, sugar, salt, and baking soda. Blend with a fork or whisk to distribute evenly. Add the milk and molasses. (To keep the molasses from sticking to your measuring cup, coat it with nonstick spray first.) Stir until well blended. Stir in the dried fruit if desired. Pour into the prepared pan and bake for about 75 minutes, or until a knife inserted into the center comes out clean.

Makes 1 loaf (eighteen 1/2-inch slices)

Orange Marmalade Bread

Marmalade makes a nice orange bread with real fruit, yet it's not too sweet. Keep in mind that it will taste like orange marmalade, which has a little bite to it. Serve it as a dessert with a little powdered sugar, in packed lunches, or with tea in the afternoon.

1 3/4 cups all-purpose flour

1/2 cup sugar

1 1/2 teaspoons baking powder

1/2 teaspoon salt

1/2 teaspoon baking soda

2 eggs

1/3 cup cooking oil

1/4 cup evaporated milk or whole milk

1 cup orange marmalade

1 cup chopped nuts or 1/2 cup currants (optional)

Preheat the oven to 350°F. Coat a 9 × 5-inch loaf pan with oil or nonstick spray.

In a medium-sized mixing bowl, combine the flour, sugar, baking powder, salt, and baking soda, whisking with a fork to distribute. In a small bowl, lightly beat the eggs with a fork. Add the oil and milk to the eggs, stirring, then pour into the flour mixture and combine. Add the marmalade and nuts or currants if desired, then stir well.

Pour the batter into the pan and bake for 60 to 65 minutes, or until a knife inserted into the center comes out clean. Let the bread stand for 10 minutes to cool. For easier slicing, wrap the bread in plastic wrap after the 10-minute cooling period.

Makes 1 loaf (eighteen 1/2-inch slices)

Peach Bread

Perfect for a summer treat or a winter pick-me-up.

One 15-ounce can sliced peaches
(in light or heavy syrup), drained

2 cups all-purpose flour

1/2 teaspoon baking soda

1/2 teaspoon salt

2 teaspoons baking powder

1 cup sugar

1/3 cup cooking oil

1 egg

1/4 cup bottled lemon juice

1 teaspoon vanilla extract

1/2 cup chopped nuts (optional)

2 to 3 tablespoons peach preserves
or marmalade (optional)

Preheat the oven to 350°F. Coat a 9 × 5-inch loaf pan with nonstick spray or cooking oil.

In a medium-sized mixing bowl, beat the peaches with an electric beater until they resemble chunky applesauce. (You want some little pieces.)

In another medium-sized mixing bowl, combine the flour, baking soda, salt, and baking powder, using a fork to stir and distribute. Add the sugar, oil, egg, lemon juice, and vanilla extract to the peaches, mixing just until blended. Add the flour mixture to the peach mixture, beating or stirring until completely moistened. Stir in the nuts if desired.

Pour the batter into the prepared pan and bake for 55 to 60 minutes, or until a knife inserted in the center of the bread comes out clean. Let stand for 10 minutes, then remove the bread from the pan. Spread marmalade or preserves on top to glaze, if desired.

Makes 1 loaf (eighteen 1/2-inch slices)

Pineapple Muffins

How often do you get pineapple muffins? They're fairly simple to make when the pineapple is already ripe and cut for you. This is another one of my grandma's recipes.

2 cups all-purpose flour	1/2 cup cooking oil
3 teaspoons baking powder	1 teaspoon vanilla extract
1 teaspoon salt	1 teaspoon bottled lemon juice
1/2 teaspoon baking soda	1 large egg
1/2 cup sugar	1/2 cup yellow raisins (or black raisins)
One 8-ounce can pineapple chunks or slices, *not* drained	

Preheat the oven to 400°F. Coat twelve muffin cups with oil or line them with muffin papers.

In a medium-sized mixing bowl, combine the flour, baking powder, salt, baking soda, and sugar, stirring well with a fork or whisk to blend.

Puree the pineapple with its juice. In another mixing bowl (the one in which you'll be using a mixer), combine the pineapple puree, oil, vanilla extract, lemon juice, and egg. Mix well, then slowly add the flour mixture, beating until well combined. Stir in the raisins.

Pour the batter into the prepared muffin cups and bake about for 15 minutes, or until a knife inserted into the centers comes out clean.

Makes 12 muffins

Tomato Soup–Spice Bread

It took me a long time to work up the courage to try a tomato soup cake recipe, but it turns out it tastes a lot like a simple spice cake, with just a touch of tartness. It's surprisingly good and is quite an easy way to obtain lycopene, a significant antioxidant.

1³/4 cups all-purpose flour

1/2 teaspoon baking soda

1/2 teaspoon salt

2 teaspoons baking powder

1 teaspoon ground cinnamon

1/2 teaspoon ground nutmeg

1/2 teaspoon ground cloves

1/2 teaspoon ground ginger

1 egg

1/3 cup cooking oil

1 teaspoon vanilla extract

1 cup sugar

One 10.75-ounce can tomato soup

1/2 cup currants or raisins

1/2 cup chopped nuts (optional)

Preheat the oven to 350°F. Lightly coat a 9 × 5-inch loaf pan with oil or nonstick spray.

In a medium-sized mixing bowl, combine the flour, baking soda, salt, baking powder, cinnamon, nutmeg, cloves, and ginger. Stir with a fork to sift and blend.

In another medium mixing bowl, lightly beat the egg, then add the oil, vanilla extract, and sugar. Beat until smooth. Alternately add batches of flour mixture and soup until all are combined and beaten smooth. Stir in the currants or raisins and nuts, if desired.

Pour into the prepared pan and bake for 45 to 50 minutes, or until a knife inserted into the center comes out clean. Cool for 10 minutes, then wrap in plastic for easier slicing.

Makes 1 loaf (eighteen ½-inch slices)

Cinnamon-Apple Pancakes

The next time you crave pancakes, try these. They're really tasty and are as easy to make as plain pancakes.

1 1/2 cups all-purpose flour

1/4 cup sugar

1 tablespoon baking powder

1 teaspoon ground cinnamon

1/2 teaspoon ground nutmeg

1/2 teaspoon salt

1/2 teaspoon baking soda

8 ounces evaporated milk or whole milk

3/4 cup applesauce

1 egg, lightly beaten

1 tablespoon cooking oil

1 teaspoon vanilla extract

Toppings (optional)

One 15-ounce can sliced apples, drained

One 20-ounce can apple pie filling

Raisins

Confectioners' sugar

Pancake syrup

Whipped topping

Chopped walnuts, pecans, or almonds

In a large mixing bowl, whisk together the flour, sugar, baking powder, cinnamon, nutmeg, salt, and baking soda. Add the remaining ingredients and stir until the batter is thoroughly moistened, taking care not to overbeat.

Prepare a large frying pan or griddle with cooking oil or nonstick spray. Place it on the stove over medium-high heat. When the pan is hot, ladle the batter about 1/4 cup at a time (I use my 1/4 cup measure as a ladle) into the frying pan, cooking only as many as comfortably fit on the pan surface. Watch for little bubbles to come to the surface of the pancake, then turn the pancakes over after the bubbles have popped. Brown the other side for about 1 1/2 minutes. Repeat until all the batter is gone.

Serve with one (or more) of the toppings listed above.

Makes about 18 pancakes (5 to 6 inches in diameter each)

Pie Crust Made with Oil

One reason I rarely make my own pie crusts is that I hate working with the cold butter (or unhealthy shortening) and trying to cut it into the flour properly. Using oil instead of butter not only eliminates that cumbersome step but also allows you to use a fat without cholesterol. And it's very fast!

1 cup plus 2 tablespoons all-purpose flour
1/2 teaspoon salt

1/4 cup cooking oil
3 tablespoons cold evaporated milk or whole milk

In a medium mixing bowl, combine the flour and salt, whisking to incorporate them. In another bowl, pour the cooking oil into the milk and, without mixing, pour the oil-milk mixture into the flour mixture all at once. Stir with a fork and make a ball out of the dough.

Using a rolling pin, roll out the dough between two pieces of waxed paper cut about 12 inches long. Roll the dough flat and smooth to the edges. If your recipe calls for an unbaked crust, the dough is ready.

If your recipe calls for a prebaked pie crust, pull one sheet of waxed paper off the dough, then place the dough (paper side up) in your pie pan. Carefully remove the remaining waxed paper and press the dough into the plate and against the sides. Pierce the dough several times with fork tines along the bottom and sides. Bake for 10 to 12 minutes, or until golden-brown.

Makes one 9-inch pie crust

Double Crust

If you need a top and bottom crust, or two pie crusts, follow the directions above but double the amount of ingredients: 2¼ cups all-purpose flour; 1 teaspoon salt; ½ cup cooking oil; and ⅓ cup cold evaporated milk or whole milk.

Make the dough as above, but split it into two balls before rolling it out.

Makes two 9-inch pie crusts

Coconut Pie Crust

This one's also very easy. Use it for custard-type pies such as chocolate cream, caramel cream, or banana cream.

2 cups flaked coconut　　　　**3 tablespoons butter, melted**

Preheat the oven to 325°F. Coat a 9-inch pie pan with oil or nonstick spray.

In a medium mixing bowl, combine the coconut and melted butter with a large spoon.

Turn the coconut mixture onto your pie pan and spread it evenly. Press the mixture into the bottom and up the sides of the pie pan to make a firm, even crust.

Bake for 15 to 18 minutes, or until the edge is golden. Cool thoroughly before filling.

Makes one 9-inch pie crust

Graham Cracker Pie Crust

You can buy graham cracker pie crusts already made at many grocery stores, but they're also quite easy to make at home. You may crush your own crackers or buy the crumbs by the box. Use this type of crust with refrigerated or frozen pie fillings. For a crispier crust, bake the crust for a few minutes first.

1¼ cups graham cracker crumbs   **¼ cup sugar** (optional)
⅓ cup (6 tablespoons) butter, melted

Combine all of the ingredients and press them firmly into the bottom and up the sides of a 9-inch pie pan.

For a crispier crust, preheat the oven to 375°F. Bake the crust for 6 to 8 minutes, then let it cool completely before filling.

Makes one 9-inch pie crust

Grandma's Easy
Homemade Biscuits

Fresh hot biscuits with butter or honey can really make a meal. It seems like we always had biscuits with breakfast or dinner at my grandma's house. She used shortening, which many people prefer not to use nowadays, though it does make for a nice flaky crust. However, you may certainly substitute oil or mayonnaise (yes, mayonnaise) for an equal amount of shortening.

3 cups all-purpose flour

4 teaspoons baking powder

1 teaspoon salt

1 tablespoon sugar

¼ cup shortening, oil, or
    mayonnaise

One 12-ounce can evaporated milk

Preheat the oven to 425°F. Coat a baking sheet with oil or nonstick spray. In a large mixing bowl, combine the flour, baking powder, salt, and sugar and stir with a fork or whisk to blend. If using shortening or mayonnaise, cut it into the flour mixture with two knives or a pastry blender so that it resembles coarse meal. Stir in the milk and blend until moistened. If using oil, combine the oil with the milk, then stir the milk-oil mixture into the flour mixture, blending until moistened (see Notes).

Dust your hands and work surface with some flour, then press the dough flat, to about ¾ inch thick. You may use round cookie or biscuit cutters, or you may pull pieces of dough out and make round "patties" with your hands. Patties or rounds should still be about ¾ inch thick.

Bake for 20 to 25 minutes, or until the biscuits are golden-brown.

Notes: The oil is added to the milk before incorporating it into the flour, whereas the shortening and mayonnaise are cut into the dry ingredients first. Just take little bits of mayonnaise and flick them into the flour, then blend it in. You may also use your hands for this.

Also, make sure your baking powder is not clumped. It's a nasty surprise to get a clod of baking powder in a biscuit, because it's quite bitter.

VARIATION

Bacon Biscuits

Follow the recipe above and add about 3 tablespoons of bottled real bacon pieces to the dough.

VARIATION

Cheese Biscuits

Follow the recipe above and add 1 cup of shredded Cheddar cheese to the dough.

VARIATION

Cheese and Bacon Biscuits

Follow the recipe above and add 1 cup of shredded Cheddar cheese and 3 tablespoons of bottled real bacon pieces to the dough.

Parmesan Rolls

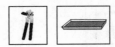

Here's an easy way to add some flavor to dinner rolls. You may substitute Cheddar cheese for Parmesan if you wish. Great with Italian or Greek meals or just to enliven a chicken dinner.

One 8-serving can refrigerated crescent roll dough
1/2 cup real grated Parmesan cheese (*not* the powdered kind)

Pinch black pepper (optional)

Preheat the oven according to the package directions.

Prepare a baking sheet with oil or nonstick spray. Prepare the rolls according to the package directions. You will have eight triangles of dough. Sprinkle about 1 tablespoon of cheese near the wide end of each triangle opposite the point. (Sprinkle a pinch of black pepper over the cheese if desired.) Roll each triangle from the wide end to the point, as shown on the dough container. Bend the rolls into half-moons. If you have extra cheese, sprinkle and gently press it onto the tops of the rolls. Bake as directed.

Serves 8

Olive Bread with Cumin and Oregano

The reason I don't make bread more often (by hand) is the yeast. I stress over getting the water warm enough to activate the yeast yet not so warm that it kills it. Then you have to wait for it to rise and knead it some more. This bread has no yeast. It's easy, and you can either place it in a 9 × 5-inch loaf pan or just make a round so it comes out looking nice and "old world." Perfect for a Greek or Italian dinner.

2¹/₂ cups all-purpose flour

1 tablespoon plus 1 teaspoon
   double-acting baking powder

¹/₂ teaspoon salt

1 tablespoon dried oregano

1 teaspoon ground cumin

1 egg, lightly beaten

1 cup evaporated milk or whole milk

2 tablespoons olive oil, plus more for
   brushing, if desired

One 2.25-ounce can sliced black
   olives, drained

1 cup chopped walnuts (optional)

Preheat the oven to 350°F. Coat a 9 × 5-inch loaf pan or a baking sheet with oil or nonstick spray.

In a medium-sized mixing bowl, combine the flour, baking powder, salt, oregano, and cumin. Stir with a fork or whisk to distribute. Add the beaten egg, milk, and oil. Stir until moistened. Stir in the olives and nuts if using.

Smooth the dough into the prepared pan, or form it into a ball shape, place it on an oiled baking sheet, and flatten it into a round about 3 inches high and 8 or 9 inches in diameter. Brush a little olive oil on the top if desired, to help browning.

Bake for about 40 minutes, or until the crust is brown and a knife inserted into the center comes out clean.

Serves 8

Potato Cashew Samosas

Here's a variation on this traditional Indian snack. It's especially good for people who don't like peas, as long as they like cashew nuts.

One 15-ounce can sliced potatoes, rinsed and drained

1 cup chopped cashew nuts

3 tablespoons currants or chopped raisins

3 tablespoons canned diced chilies (mild, or hot if you like it spicy)

2 tablespoons bottled lemon juice

1 tablespoon soy sauce

1 tablespoon ground coriander

1 teaspoon ground cumin

1 teaspoon chili powder

¼ teaspoon ground cinnamon

4 cans refrigerated crescent rolls

Preheat oven to 400°F. Prepare a baking sheet with a light coat of oil or nonstick spray. Dice potatoes. Combine potatoes, nuts, raisins, chilies, lemon juice, and soy sauce in a medium-sized mixing bowl. In a small bowl, whisk together coriander, cumin, chili powder, and cinnamon, then add to the potato mixture. Toss to coat.

Separate dough triangles. Spoon potato mixture onto one triangle, filling as much as you can but leaving space at all the edges. Place another dough triangle over the top of that one and crimp all the edges together. When sealed, gently place the samosa on your prepared baking sheet. Repeat for all. Bake 12 to 15 minutes, or until golden brown.

Makes 16 samosas

Pasta and Rice

CHAPTER 8

Baked Ziti

I am all about not waiting for water to boil. With this recipe you don't need to boil the pasta separately. Just mix everything in a bowl and then bake. Now *that's* comfort food.

One 26-ounce jar spaghetti sauce

One 16-ounce container sour cream
(reduced-fat is okay)

One 14-ounce can beef broth or 1 cube/teaspoon beef or vegetable bouillon dissolved in 1³/4 cups hot water

1 cup shredded mozzarella or Jack cheese

1 cup shredded real Parmesan cheese
(*not* the powdered kind)

16 ounces ziti or other tube pasta, such as small macaroni

Preheat the oven to 400°F.

In a large mixing bowl, combine the spaghetti sauce with the sour cream. Stir in the broth. Add ½ cup of mozzarella or Jack cheese and ½ cup Parmesan cheese. Stir in the pasta and blend well. Pour into a 9 × 13-inch baking dish, cover with foil, and bake for 1 hour.

Remove the baking dish from the oven, uncover (carefully—watch out for very hot steam), and sprinkle with the remaining cheeses. Return the dish to the oven without a cover and bake for 10 more minutes, or until the cheese is melted.

Serves 8

Penne with Spicy Tomato-Cheese Sauce

This is a very easy sauce to put together and a tasty way to go meatless if you like cheese.

16 ounces penne or other tube-shaped pasta

One 28-ounce can tomato puree

One 28-ounce can diced tomatoes

2 teaspoons sugar

1 teaspoon garlic powder

1 teaspoon dried basil

1 teaspoon salt (optional)

1 teaspoon dried red pepper flakes (or 1/2 teaspoon cayenne)

1/2 teaspoon onion powder

1/2 teaspoon dried oregano

2 cups shredded Cheddar cheese

1 cup shredded real Parmesan cheese (*not* the powdered kind)

Canned sliced olives or sliced mushrooms as desired (optional)

Cook the pasta according to the package directions.

In a medium saucepan, combine the remaining ingredients and cook over medium heat, stirring periodically. The sauce is ready when it's hot and the cheese is almost completely melted.

Serve one of two ways:

Combine cooked, drained pasta with sauce and toss to coat.

Or serve sauce over cooked, drained pasta.

Serves 8

Fettuccine with Tomato and Walnuts

Here's a nice pasta dish if you're looking to go Italian but meatless. The cheese in the sauce adds some protein, and if you add beans to the pasta (a grain), you'll get the complete amino-acid chain for even more protein.

16 ounces fettuccine, linguine, or tagliatelle

One 28-ounce can whole peeled tomatoes, *not* drained

One 15-ounce can onions, *not* drained

1/4 cup white wine or 1 tablespoon rice vinegar plus 3 tablespoons water

1 teaspoon balsamic vinegar

1 teaspoon dried basil

1/2 teaspoon salt

1/2 teaspoon dried rosemary leaves

1/2 teaspoon garlic powder

3 tablespoons cornstarch dissolved in a little cold water

1 cup real grated Parmesan cheese (*not* the powdered kind), plus extra for garnish

1 tablespoon cooking oil (such as olive)

1 cup chopped walnuts

Prepare the pasta according to the package directions. While you're waiting for the pasta water to boil, make the sauce:

Pour the juice from the tomato can into a medium-sized nonreactive saucepan. Coarsely chop the tomatoes and add them to the juice. Add the onions with juice, wine or rice vinegar, balsamic vinegar, basil, salt, rosemary, garlic powder, and cornstarch mixture to the saucepan, and bring to a boil. Add the Parmesan cheese and stir. Continue heating while the sauce thickens. You may let it simmer while you prepare other things.

Before serving time, pour the oil into a small pan and add the walnuts, stirring to coat. Cook over medium-low heat for about 5 minutes, stirring to keep the nuts from burning. Meanwhile, combine the finished pasta with the tomato sauce and toss to coat. Serve with walnuts and extra Parmesan on top.

Serves 8

Spaghetti with Roasted Red Pepper and Zucchini Sauce

Roasted red peppers impart an unusual flavor to this red pasta sauce. Be sure you don't use an aluminum saucepan, as it may react with the acids in the tomato sauce and peppers.

16 ounces spaghetti, linguine, or
   fettuccine
One 12-ounce jar roasted red
   peppers
One 8-ounce can tomato sauce
One 14.5-ounce can chicken broth
One 14.5-ounce can zucchini in
   Italian tomato sauce

1 teaspoon sugar
1/2 teaspoon salt
1/2 teaspoon dried thyme
1/4 teaspoon garlic powder
1/4 teaspoon onion powder
1/4 teaspoon ground black pepper
Shredded real Parmesan cheese for
   garnish (*not* the powdered kind)

Cook the pasta according to the package directions. Drain the roasted red peppers and puree them. The puree should be a little chunky.

Combine the puree with the tomato sauce, chicken broth, zucchini, sugar, salt, thyme, garlic powder, onion powder, and black pepper in a saucepan. Stir to combine, then bring the mixture to a low boil. When hot, serve over pasta and garnish with Parmesan cheese.

Serves 8 to 10

Pasta with Lemon, Basil, Olives, and Beans

Here's a way to get vegetables and legumes with your grains. This may be served as a meal, a first course, or a side dish.

2 tablespoons butter

1/4 cup olive oil or other vegetable oil

1/4 cup bottled lemon juice

1 teaspoon dried basil

1/2 teaspoon garlic powder

1/2 teaspoon salt

1/2 teaspoon onion powder

1/4 teaspoon dried oregano

Two 4-ounce cans sliced black olives, drained

One 15-ounce can kidney beans or other beans, rinsed and drained

One 15-ounce can cut green beans, drained

One 7-ounce can sliced mushrooms, drained (optional)

One 8-ounce can sliced carrots, drained (optional)

8 ounces pasta such as linguine, egg noodles, or rotini

Shredded real Parmesan cheese (*not the powdered kind*) for garnish

In a medium saucepan, combine the butter, oil, lemon juice, basil, garlic powder, salt, onion powder, and oregano. Stir, then cook over medium heat until the butter has melted. Add the olives, beans, and other vegetables, if using, toss to coat, and cook for a couple of minutes.

Meanwhile, prepare the pasta in a large pot according to the package directions. When the pasta is finished and drained, place it back in your large pot. Pour the lemon-vegetable mixture on top of the pasta and toss to mix and coat.

Sprinkle Parmesan cheese on the pasta as desired and toss, or bring a bowl of Parmesan for individual use at the table.

Serves 6

Spicy Noodle and Cashew Stir-Fry

This is a nice change of pace for noodle dishes. It may be used as a main meatless dish or as a side dish for Asian cuisine. If you don't find the stir-fried vegetables at your store, don't worry: I'm giving you the separate equivalents, too.

8 ounces packaged thin noodles,
such as spaghetti

1/4 cup cooking oil (preferably peanut or
sesame)

1/4 teaspoon cayenne

1 cup cashews

Two 28-ounce cans stir-fried
vegetables *or*:

two 15-ounce cans bean sprouts,
drained

two 8-ounce cans bamboo shoots,
drained

one 8-ounce can sliced water
chestnuts, drained

1/2 cup chopped roasted red
peppers from a jar

one 15-ounce can small baby
corn-on-the-cob, drained

one 8-ounce can sliced carrots,
drained

3/4 cup teriyaki sauce

Cook the noodles according to the package directions, then drain.

Put the oil in a wok or frying pan over medium heat. Add the cayenne and cook for about 1 minute. Add the cashews and cook for another minute. Add the vegetables, stirring so they're coated with oil, and cooking them until they are hot. Stir in the noodles and toss to coat. Add the teriyaki sauce, toss to coat, and continue to cook until the noodles are heated. Serve hot.

Serves 8

Thai Lime-Peanut Noodles

This is an easy side dish that would go well with any Asian-themed meal. Try it with fish, chicken, or pork main courses.

8 ounces egg noodles, spaghetti, or other pasta

1/2 cup creamy peanut butter

1 tablespoon plus 2 teaspoons bottled lime juice

1 tablespoon peanut oil or other cooking oil

1 teaspoon soy sauce

1/2 teaspoon garlic powder

1/2 teaspoon onion powder

1/2 teaspoon ground ginger

1/2 teaspoon ground coriander

1/4 teaspoon cayenne

1/2 cup chopped peanuts (optional)

Prepare the noodles according to the package directions.

Meanwhile, in a small mixing bowl, combine the peanut butter, 1/2 cup of water (see Note), 1 tablespoon of lime juice, the cooking oil, and the soy sauce. Whisk with a fork until creamy. Add the garlic powder, onion powder, ginger, coriander, and cayenne, and whisk until blended.

When the noodles are done, drained, and still hot, place them in a medium mixing bowl. Add the peanut sauce and toss to coat. (It won't be like a spaghetti sauce; it will be more of a coating.) Add the remaining 2 teaspoons of lime juice, toss, and serve. Sprinkle with chopped peanuts if desired.

Serves 4

Note: If sauce seems too thick to toss with noodles, add another 1/4 cup water.

Creamy Parmesan Rice

This makes a lovely side dish for chicken, fish, or Italian-themed meals.

1 cup rice (or 2 cups instant rice)

One 12-ounce can evaporated milk
  or 1¹/₂ cups whole milk

1 tablespoon cornstarch dissolved in
  a little cold water

2 tablespoons butter

1 teaspoon salt

1 cup shredded real Parmesan cheese
  (*not* the powdered kind)

Prepare the rice according to the package directions.

To make the sauce, whisk together the milk and dissolved cornstarch in a medium-sized saucepan. Add the butter and salt and stir over medium-high heat. When the butter has melted, add the cheese. Stir until the cheese has melted and the sauce has thickened (just a few minutes).

When the rice is ready, combine the rice and sauce and stir well.

Serves 6

VARIATION

Creamy Parmesan Rice with Lemon and Herbs

Follow the directions above. While the rice is still hot, add 1 tablespoon of bottled lemon juice, 1 tea-spoon of ground sage, 1 teaspoon of dried parsley, and ¹/₄ teaspoon of ground black pepper. Stir well.

Herbed Orange Rice

This rice is good with poultry, pork, or Asian-themed meals.

1 cup rice (or 2 cups instant rice)

1 cup orange juice

1 teaspoon dried marjoram

1/2 teaspoon ground sage

1/2 teaspoon dried basil

1/2 teaspoon salt

1 tablespoon butter (optional)

Prepare the rice according to the package directions, but substitute the cup of orange juice plus 1 cup of water for the the liquid called for in the directions. Add the marjoram, sage, basil, and salt. When the rice is done, stir in the butter if desired.

Serves 6

Minted Rice

This is a great side for any type of Middle Eastern or Greek food and stands in very well for couscous.

1 cup rice	**1 tablespoon butter**
One 14-ounce can chicken broth	**2 to 3 teaspoons dried mint**

Prepare the rice according to the package directions, substituting the chicken broth plus ¼ cup water for the water. When the rice is finished, stir in the butter until melted, then stir in the mint.

Serves 6

VARIATION

Minted Cilantro Rice

Follow the recipe above, adding 2 teaspoons of dried cilantro flakes with the mint.

Note: These rice dishes taste even better over time (as leftovers), after the flavors have had even more time to develop.

Cheesy Spanish Rice

I love the tartness provided by the salsa in this dish. The salsa I always use has cilantro in it, which I love. If your salsa doesn't have any, you might want to add some. You can also add a can of chicken to this rice for a complete meal.

2 cups long-grain rice	2 cups prepared salsa, divided
1 1/2 cups shredded Cheddar cheese, divided	One 15-ounce can corn, drained
1 1/2 cups shredded Jack cheese, divided	1 cup sour cream (low-fat is okay)

Preheat the oven to 350°F.

Prepare the rice according to the package directions. When the rice is done, combine it with 1 cup of the Cheddar cheese, 1 cup of the Jack cheese, 1 cup of the prepared salsa, all the corn, and the sour cream.

Spread the rice mixture into a 9 × 13-inch pan. Pour the remaining cup of salsa over the top, spreading it as evenly as you can. Top with the remaining cheese. Bake 20 to 25 minutes, or until heated through.

Serves 8

Tex-Mex Rice

This is sort of a mild hodgepodge with Southwestern leanings. It's great for kids or those who aren't fond of spicy foods. If you want to add some zip, try a pinch of cayenne.

1 cup long-grain rice	**One 2.25-ounce can sliced black**
1 teaspoon/cube chicken bouillon	**olives, drained**
One 15-ounce can diced tomatoes	**Salt and pepper**
One 15-ounce can corn, drained	**Cayenne** (optional)

Prepare the rice according to the package directions, adding the bouillon to the cooking water. When the rice is done, stir in the tomatoes with their juice, corn, olives, salt and pepper to taste, and cayenne, if using.

Serves 6

Pulao (Indian Rice)

I love the rice you get in Indian restaurants. This version is much, much faster. (And it doesn't involve saffron. Have you priced real saffron lately? Yikes!) I think you'll find it a nice side dish or a wonderful rice to serve with a curry. Try it with the Chicken and Potato Curry on page 88.

One 14-ounce can chicken broth
   plus 1/4 cup water, or
   1 cube/teaspoon vegetable or
   chicken bouillon dissolved in
   2 cups water
1 cup basmati or other long-grain
   rice
1 tablespoon curry powder
1 teaspoon onion powder
1 teaspoon sugar

3/4 teaspoon ground cumin
1/4 teaspoon garlic powder
1/4 teaspoon salt
1/4 teaspoon ground cinnamon
1 tablespoon butter
One 15-ounce can peas-and-carrots
   blend (optional)
1/2 cup coarsely chopped cashews or
   almonds
1/4 cup golden or black raisins

Put the broth or the dissolved bouillon in a medium saucepan and bring to a boil. Add the rice and cook according to the package directions.

Meanwhile, in a small bowl, blend the curry powder, onion powder, sugar, cumin, garlic powder, salt, and cinnamon.

When the rice is cooked, add the butter and stir until melted. Add the spice mixture and blend well. Gently stir in the vegetables if using, then add the nuts and raisins.

Serves 6

Vegetables

CHAPTER 9

Sautéed Artichokes

These 'chokes cook up fast and make a great side to chicken, fish, or Italian foods. Be sure to get artichoke bottoms that have not been canned with vinegar, as they can be a bit tart. If you can't find artichoke bottoms, you may use quartered artichoke hearts instead, as long as they haven't been packed in vinegar.

One 14-ounce can artichoke
   bottoms, drained
2 tablespoons olive oil
1/2 teaspoon onion powder
1/2 teaspoon garlic powder
1/8 teaspoon salt

1 to 2 tablespoons white wine
   (optional)
2 tablespoons shredded real
   Parmesan cheese (*not* the powdered
   kind; optional)

Drain the artichokes and slice the whole bottoms in two. Pour the olive oil into a medium-sized frying pan. Turn the heat to medium and add the onion powder, garlic powder, salt, and white wine (if using). Stir, then add the cut artichokes. Sauté until they are hot and then serve. If using Parmesan, remove the pan from the heat and sprinkle the cheese over the artichokes in the pan. Let the cheese melt a little before serving.

Serves 3

Greek Green Beans

This one's super simple but tastes like you went to a lot of trouble for a side dish. It's even good without the cheese.

2 tablespoons olive oil

1 1/2 teaspoons dried oregano

1 teaspoon onion powder

1/2 teaspoon garlic powder

Pinch salt

One 15-ounce can diced tomatoes, *not* drained

1/4 teaspoon sugar

Two 15-ounce cans cut green beans, drained

One 2.25-ounce can sliced black olives, drained

Feta cheese (optional)

Place the olive oil in a medium saucepan. Add the oregano, onion powder, garlic powder, and salt, then stir over medium heat for a minute or so, until fragrant. Add the tomatoes with their juice, then sprinkle the sugar over the tomatoes (it helps cut any sharpness) and stir. Add the green beans and olives, stir, and gently simmer for about 5 minutes to let the flavors ripen.

Serve with crumbled feta cheese on top as desired.

Serves 6

Dilled Green Beans

I call for a relatively small quantity of dill in this dish because I find it can be overpowering, but please feel free to add more if you'd like. Makes a nice accompaniment to meat, fish, or Greek foods.

One 15-ounce can green beans, *not* drained

1/4 teaspoon onion powder

1/4 teaspoon salt

1 teaspoon dried dill

Pour the green beans with their liquid into a saucepan. Add the onion powder, salt, and dill, and heat to boiling. Let the beans sit a few minutes before serving to allow the flavors to develop.

(Alternately, you may also heat the entire contents in the microwave using a microwave-safe container.)

Serves 3

Green Beans Amandine

Here's a very fast way to dress up ordinary green beans. They taste great and you can easily double the recipe to accommodate more people.

One 15-ounce can green beans (any style), ***not*** **drained**

2 tablespoons butter

1 teaspoon bottled lemon juice

1/4 cup chopped almonds

Salt and pepper

Heat the green beans in their liquid until they're nice and hot. In a separate bowl or pan, melt the butter and stir the lemon juice into it.

Drain the green beans and place them in a serving bowl. Pour the lemon butter over the beans. Add the chopped almonds and toss everything together to coat. Add salt and pepper to taste.

Serves 3

Southern Succotash

Succotash is a simple yet tasty dish and has the added nutritional benefit of combining a grain and legume to give you the entire amino acid chain for a complete protein. Some succotash recipes call for milk (which you may add here if you wish) or a cream sauce. I prefer simpler recipes like this one, both in terms of taste and ease of preparation (and the reduced calories).

One 15-ounce can corn, drained

One 15-ounce can lima beans or butter beans, drained

2 tablespoons butter

Salt and pepper

Heat the vegetables with the butter, using either a skillet over medium heat or a microwave oven on medium-high setting. They're ready when the butter has melted and the vegetables are hot enough for your taste. Salt and pepper as desired, then serve.

Serves 6

Green Bean Succotash

Succotash is usually made with corn and lima beans, but you can use green beans, too. If you prefer a creamy succotash, use cream-style corn in place of regular corn.

One 15-ounce can green beans

One 15-ounce can corn (drained) or **cream-style corn**

1 tablespoon butter (optional if using cream-style corn)

Regular Corn Method with Butter

For succotash with butter, heat the beans and corn together. When hot, drain the vegetables and add butter.

Cream-Style Corn Method

For creamy succotash, drain the green beans and heat with the cream-style corn. Add butter if desired.

Serves 6

Tex-Mex Spiced Black Beans

Black beans make a great side dish for Mexican or Cuban fare. It's easy to add a little flair with a few spices.

One 15-ounce can black beans,
drained (*not* rinsed)
1/2 teaspoon ground cumin

1/2 teaspoon dried oregano
1/4 teaspoon onion powder

Combine all of the ingredients and heat as desired.

Serves 3

Homemade Vegetarian Chili

I've noticed that some cans of ready-made chili have several additives. I like making my own since I know there's nothing like that in it. And this hearty chili is a breeze to make.

Two 15-ounce cans kidney or pinto beans, rinsed and drained

One 15-ounce can diced tomatoes in juice, *not* drained

One 15-ounce can tomato sauce

2 tablespoons plus 1 teaspoon chili powder

1 teaspoon onion powder

1 teaspoon sugar

1 teaspoon ground cumin

1/2 teaspoon garlic powder

1/2 teaspoon dried oregano

1/4 teaspoon salt

Ground black pepper (optional)

Combine all of the ingredients, then heat. (You may heat it in the microwave, or use a saucepan over the stove. Just be sure not to use an aluminum pan, as it can cause an acidic taste in the tomatoes.)

Serves 4

Falafel with Minted Yogurt Sauce

Falafel is basically bean cakes made from garbanzo beans (also known as chickpeas). This is an easy way to make homemade falafel because you're starting with ready-to-use beans. You can serve falafel as an appetizer, on a salad, or as a sandwich in a pita pocket with tomato, cucumber, and lettuce. See recipe for minted Yogurt Sauce on page 258.

**Two 16-ounce cans garbanzo beans,
   rinsed and drained**

1 tablespoon olive oil (optional)

2 eggs

1 1/2 teaspoons onion powder

1 1/2 teaspoons garlic powder

1 1/2 teaspoons ground cumin

1 teaspoon dried oregano

1/2 teaspoon ground coriander

1/2 teaspoon salt

1/4 teaspoon ground black pepper

Olive oil for pan-frying

1/3 cup bread crumbs

Minted Yogurt Sauce (see page 258)

Process the garbanzo beans with a hand blender or food processor until mostly smooth. If the beans seem dry and difficult to blend, add a tablespoon of olive oil. Lightly beat the eggs, then stir into the beans and mix well.

Combine the onion powder, garlic powder, cumin, oregano, coriander, salt, and pepper, then mix in with the beans. Form the bean mixture into balls roughly 1 to 2 inches in diameter (you'll get sixteen to eighteen), and place them on a piece of waxed paper.

Pour about ¼ inch of oil in a frying pan and place over medium heat. Coat the bean balls in bread crumbs, then place them in the hot skillet. Flatten them a little in the pan with a spatula. Turn the patties over after the bottoms brown. Add oil as necessary for even browning. Serve with Minted Yogurt Sauce.

Makes 16 to 18 patties

Middle Eastern Beets

It may seem a little strange to put beets and yogurt together, but if you like Middle Eastern fare and sauces made from a yogurt base, you'll probably like beets prepared this way. The thing about beets is that everything turns pink. If you can live with that, you'll be okay with this dish. In fact, it might be nice to serve for a holiday or even Valentine's Day.

1 cup plain yogurt (nonfat is okay)

¼ teaspoon salt

¼ teaspoon ground black pepper

¼ teaspoon garlic powder

¼ teaspoon onion powder

⅛ teaspoon ground cinnamon

One 15-ounce can sliced or julienne-
   cut beets, drained

Combine the yogurt, salt, pepper, garlic powder, onion powder, and ground cinnamon. Whisk with a fork until smooth.

After draining beets as best you can, add them to the yogurt mixture. Serve cold, or heat to desired temperature.

Serves 3

Indian-Spiced Corn

Corn is a great side dish and stays nice and firm through the canning process. Here's a way to add some zip to this favorite. (And this recipe is easily doubled.)

2 tablespoons olive oil or other
cooking oil

2 teaspoons onion powder

1 teaspoon ground cumin

1/2 teaspoon garlic powder

1/2 teaspoon ground coriander

1/2 teaspoon bottled lemon juice

Pinch salt

One 15-ounce can corn, drained

Place the olive oil in a medium saucepan over medium heat. Add the onion powder, cumin, garlic powder, coriander, lemon juice, and salt. Cook, stirring, for about a minute, until the mixture becomes fragrant and blended. Add the corn and stir to coat. Heat for just another minute or until the corn is hot.

Serves 3

Sweet Corn and Roasted Red Peppers

Roasted red peppers (from a jar) add a nice bit of color to corn. This dish makes a great side for Mexican or Southwestern fare.

One 15-ounce can corn

1/3 cup diced roasted red peppers

(from a jar)

1 tablespoon butter (optional if cooking

on the stove)

Salt and pepper

Microwave Method:

Drain the corn, then combine it with the peppers and butter in a medium-sized microwave-safe bowl. Heat to desired temperature (about a minute on high will more than do it).

Stovetop Method:

Empty the corn and its liquid into a saucepan and heat over medium-high heat until hot. Drain the hot corn, then add the red peppers and butter, if using.

Serves 4

Cheesy Hominy and Sour Cream

Hominy is simply corn that's been processed differently from regular corn. This is a very easy side dish, with the sour cream lending a tart note to the hominy, which can be a little bland if not paired with stronger flavors.

Try using a mixture of Cheddar and Jack cheeses. If you substitute one can of kidney beans for one can of hominy, you'll get the complete amino-acid chain for a protein.

One 16-ounce container sour cream

1 1/2 teaspoons onion powder

1 teaspoon garlic powder

1/2 teaspoon salt

Two 15-ounce cans hominy (white or
   yellow), drained, or one 15-ounce
   can hominy and one 15-ounce can
   kidney beans, rinsed and drained

One or two 5-ounce cans ham,
   drained and diced (optional)

1 1/2 to 2 cups shredded Jack,
   Cheddar, or Parmesan cheese

3 tablespoons cornstarch dissolved
   in a little cold water

In a medium-sized saucepan, combine the sour cream with the onion powder, garlic powder, and salt. Mix thoroughly. Add the remaining ingredients and stir over medium heat until thick. (Thickening begins in earnest when you reach a low boil.)

Serves 6

Greek Potatoes

Simple and delicious, these potatoes make a great side to many meat or salad dishes. Use olive oil both for its flavor and to receive its cholesterol-lowering benefits.

**Two 15-ounce cans sliced potatoes,
  drained**

**2 to 3 tablespoons olive oil or other
  cooking oil**

1/2 teaspoon onion powder

1/4 teaspoon salt

1/4 teaspoon ground black pepper

1/4 teaspoon garlic powder

1 teaspoon dried oregano

Drain and rinse the potatoes to remove extra starch. Heat the olive oil in a frying pan over medium heat. When hot, add the potatoes and season with the remaining ingredients. Turn the potatoes periodically and cook until they are thoroughly heated and beginning to brown. You may cover the pan to speed cooking.

Serves 6

New Potatoes in Sour Cream and Dill

This is a simple but delicious dish that can be made in the microwave if you don't want to heat the house in the process. You can cut calories by using nonfat sour cream.

3/4 cup sour cream

1 teaspoon onion powder

1/4 teaspoon dried dill

1/4 teaspoon salt

1/4 teaspoon ground black pepper

2 tablespoons real grated Parmesan cheese (*not* the powdered kind)

Two 15-ounce cans whole potatoes, rinsed and drained

In a medium saucepan, whisk together the sour cream, onion powder, dill, salt, pepper, and cheese. Add the potatoes and toss to coat thoroughly. Cook over medium heat, stirring to keep the cream from burning. The potatoes are ready when they're heated through.

Serves 6

Creamy Mashed Potato Casserole

Yep, we're using canned potatoes here, and they work really well. Think of it as having a head start, with the potatoes already boiled and sliced for you to mash.

Three 15-ounce cans sliced potatoes, drained and rinsed
1 cup sour cream or plain yogurt
1 teaspoon onion powder
1/2 teaspoon garlic powder

1/4 teaspoon salt
1 egg
1 cup grated Cheddar or real Parmesan cheese

Preheat the oven to 350°F. Lightly coat an 8 × 8-inch baking dish with vegetable oil or non-stick spray.

Process the potatoes with a hand blender, food processor, or regular blender. You might have a few little chunks, which is fine (it gives the dish a little body).

In a small mixing bowl, combine the sour cream or yogurt, onion powder, garlic powder, salt, and egg until well blended. Add the sour cream mixture to the mashed potatoes, then stir well. Empty the mixture into the prepared baking dish and smooth the top. Sprinkle with grated cheese and bake for 20 to 25 minutes, or until the cheese has melted and the potatoes are hot.

Serves 6

Sweet Potatoes
with Caramel Sauce

Try this for a different take on candied yams during the holidays. It's delicious, and it's a time-honored tradition whipped up in minutes.

**One 29-ounce can sweet potatoes or
    yams, drained**
**¼ cup homemade Caramel Syrup
    (page 253) or store-bought caramel
    syrup**

**1 tablespoon butter, at room
    temperature**

Preheat the oven to 425°F. Lightly coat an 8 × 8-inch baking dish with oil or nonstick spray. Place the sweet potatoes in the baking dish. Perforate any large potato pieces with a fork or knife.

Combine the syrup and butter in a microwave-safe cup or bowl. Heat on high power for about 35 seconds, remove, and stir until blended completely. Heat for an additional 5 or 10 seconds on high if needed, to blend completely.

Pour the mixture evenly over the sweet potatoes and bake for 25 minutes.

Serves 6

Sweet Potato Gratin

Here's a twist on an old standby. Try serving it around the holidays as well.

Two 29-ounce cans sweet potatoes or
  yams
One 12-ounce can evaporated milk
  (nonfat is okay)
1 tablespoon butter
¼ teaspoon salt

⅛ teaspoon black pepper
2 tablespoons cornstarch, dissolved
  in a little cold water
¾ cup real Parmesan cheese,
  shredded

Preheat oven to 350°F. Lightly coat an 8 × 8-inch baking dish with oil or nonstick spray. Rinse and drain the sweet potatoes and spread them in the baking dish.

In a medium saucepan, mix evaporated milk with butter, salt, and pepper and bring to a boil, stirring frequently as milk heats. Add cornstarch and stir a couple minutes more until thickened into a sauce. Pour sauce over sweet potatoes to cover. Sprinkle Parmesan cheese over all and bake for 15 minutes.

Serves 6 to 8

Tomatoes with Basil and Oregano

This dish makes a nice side for pastas in white or cream sauces or for red meat or poultry.

One 29-ounce can whole peeled
tomatoes, *not* drained

1 teaspoon dried basil

1/2 teaspoon dried oregano

1/4 teaspoon salt (more if desired)

1/4 teaspoon ground black pepper

1/4 teaspoon sugar

1/4 cup bread crumbs

1/4 cup real grated Parmesan cheese
(*not* the powdered kind)

Pour the tomatoes with their juice into a medium-sized saucepan and cook over medium heat. Add the basil, oregano, salt, pepper, and sugar, and toss to coat.

Combine the bread crumbs and cheese in a small bowl. When the tomatoes have reached a low boil, sprinkle the bread-crumb mixture over them. Cover and remove from the heat. The cheese will melt a little, which is desired.

Serves 6

Eggs and Cheese

CHAPTER 10

Santa Fe Pizza

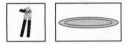

Some would argue that pizza is the perfect food. With the addition of some vegetables for nutrition, perhaps they're right. Consider using the remaining corn, beans, and chilies mixed together as a side dish. If you're using pizza dough rather than a prebaked crust, you should use a pizza pan, as it's perforated and will help the crust bake through the bottom.

One ready-made pizza crust or dough

One 8-ounce can tomato sauce

1/2 teaspoon sugar

1/4 teaspoon garlic powder

1/4 teaspoon onion powder

1/4 teaspoon chili powder

1/4 teaspoon ground cumin

2 cups shredded Jack, mozzarella, or Cheddar cheese (or mix them)

Half of one 15-ounce can black, kidney, or pinto beans, rinsed and drained

Half of one 15-ounce can corn, drained

One 2.25-ounce can sliced black olives, drained

1/3 cup diced roasted red peppers from a jar

2 tablespoons mild canned diced chilies (optional)

Preheat the oven to 450°F (or as pizza crust directions indicate). Prepare the pizza crust according to the package directions.

In a small bowl, combine the tomato sauce, sugar, garlic powder, onion powder, chili powder, and cumin. Spread the seasoned tomato sauce on the pizza crust, reaching almost to the edges. Sprinkle the cheese evenly over the sauce. Sprinkle the remaining ingredients onto the cheese.

Bake for 12 to 15 minutes, or until the crust is browned and the cheese has melted.

Serves 8

Barbecued Chicken Pizza

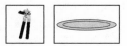

This is one of my favorite fast foods and is always a crowd pleaser. It makes a nice relaxed Friday night dinner or a perfect snacking food for The Big Game.

1 ready-made pizza crust or dough

1 cup prepared pizza sauce (or see the recipe on page 251)

2 cups shredded Parmesan, mozzarella, or Jack cheese

1/3 cup ketchup

1 tablespoon prepared mustard

2 teaspoons brown sugar

2 teaspoons pancake syrup or molasses

1/4 teaspoon garlic powder

1/4 teaspoon onion powder

1/4 teaspoon salt

1/8 to 1/4 teaspoon cayenne

1/4 to 1/2 teaspoon Liquid Smoke® (or similar condiment; optional)

One 6-ounce can white chunk chicken, rinsed, drained, and flaked

Preheat the oven to 450°F (or as pizza crust directions indicate). Prepare the pizza crust according to the package directions.

Spread the pizza sauce on the dough, leaving a 1/4-inch space along the perimeter. Sprinkle the cheese over the sauce.

In a medium-sized mixing bowl, combine the ketchup, mustard, brown sugar, syrup, garlic powder, onion powder, salt, cayenne, and Liquid Smoke®. Stir to blend. Add the chicken, then drop the chicken-sauce mixture by forkfuls onto the cheese topping.

Bake for 12 to 15 minutes, or until the crust is browned and the cheese has melted.

Serves 8

Cheese Strata

This dish makes a nice brunch or dinner meal. Usually recipes like this call for you to let the bread soak at least an hour in the egg mix before baking. They also call for day-old bread. But if you want to bake immediately, neither step is necessary if you use regular bread and push it down so that egg mix covers it. If you want to assemble the dish ahead of time and bake it later, however, you can store it in the refrigerator. If you do so, be sure to cover the dish.

6 to 8 slices bread (depending on size)

**8 prewrapped Swiss or American
    cheese slices**

4 eggs

One 12-ounce can evaporated milk

2 teaspoons onion powder

1/2 teaspoon prepared mustard

1/2 teaspoon salt

1/4 teaspoon garlic powder

1/8 teaspoon ground black pepper

Paprika for dusting the top

Preheat the oven to 350°F.

Coat an 8 × 8-inch baking pan with a little oil or nonstick spray. Line the pan with three or four pieces of bread. (You may remove the crusts first if you wish; you may also slice them any way you wish to make them fit.) Place the cheese slices on top of the bread slices. Cover the cheese with the remaining bread slices.

In a medium mixing bowl, beat the eggs, milk, 1 cup of water, onion powder, mustard, salt, garlic powder, and pepper until combined. Pour the egg mixture over the bread and cheese in the pan. Press the bread down into the liquid until it's good and moist. Sprinkle with a light dusting of paprika. Store to cook later, or bake immediately, uncovered, for about 60 minutes, or until a knife inserted into the center comes out clean. (You may get a little melted cheese on the knife, but it's still ready as long as the egg has firmed.)

Serves 6

Baked Cornbread Chiles Rellenos

I like chiles rellenos, but I usually find them a little bland, so I bake them in a cornbread batter instead of frying them in the usual flour/milk batter. This recipe also makes a small cornbread loaf to accompany the meal. Consider serving this dish with a side of black beans to provide the entire amino-acid chain for protein without using meat.

1½ cups all-purpose flour	⅓ cup cooking oil
1½ cups cornmeal	One 1-pound brick Jack cheese
½ cup sugar	One 27-ounce can whole green
2 tablespoons baking powder	chilies, drained
1 teaspoon salt	Salsa and sour cream for garnish
3 eggs	(optional)
One 12-ounce can evaporated milk	

Preheat the oven to 425°F. Coat a 9 × 13-inch baking dish and a 9 × 5-inch loaf pan with cooking oil or nonstick spray.

In a large mixing bowl, combine the flour, cornmeal, sugar, baking powder, and salt, stirring well. Add the eggs, milk, and cooking oil, and stir until moist (don't overbeat).

Cut the cheese into sixteen slices. Fill each drained chili with a slice of cheese (slice the cheese smaller or slit the pepper if you need to). Drop a chili into the corn batter to coat, then place it in the 9 × 13-inch dish. Repeat with all the chilies. Pour the remaining corn batter into the 9 × 5-inch pan. Bake both together for about 25 minutes, or until the cornbread begins to brown a little and a knife inserted into the center of the loaf comes out clean.

Serves 8

Corn Pie

This dish is a great side for Southwestern, Southern, or Mexican foods. To add some zing, throw in a 4-ounce can of diced chilies (drained).

1/2 cup butter (1 stick)

1 1/2 cups plain bread crumbs

One 12-ounce can evaporated milk

1 tablespoon cornstarch, dissolved in a little cold water

2 eggs

1 teaspoon onion powder

1/2 teaspoon salt

1/8 teaspoon nutmeg

1/8 teaspoon cayenne (optional)

One 15-ounce can corn, drained

One 4-ounce can diced green chilies, drained (optional)

Preheat oven to 375°F. Lightly coat a 9-inch pie pan with nonstick spray or cooking oil.

Melt the butter. In a medium-sized mixing bowl, thoroughly combine the melted butter with the bread crumbs. Set aside about 1/2 cup of the bread crumb mixture and press the remaining crumbs into the pie pan, forming a crust.

In a medium saucepan, combine the evaporated milk and dissolved cornstarch. Whisk in the eggs and blend thoroughly. Add the onion powder, salt, nutmeg, and cayenne, if using. Set saucepan over medium heat, stirring often to keep the eggs blended with the milk. Do not bring the mixture to a boil or your eggs may curdle. Instead, heat the mixture enough that little bubbles ring the pan, and cook it for about 5 minutes, or until thickened. Remove from the heat and add corn and chilies, if desired.

Pour the mixture into the pie crust, then sprinkle the remaining buttered bread crumbs over the top. Bake for about 30 minutes, or until a knife inserted into the center comes out clean.

Serves 6

Creamy Three-Cheese Quiche

Just when I thought quiches couldn't get easier, I discovered, through a failed soufflé, that a blender works magic with some egg dishes. This one practically melts in your mouth.

1 ready-made 9-inch pie crust (or
    follow the recipe on page 157)
4 eggs
1 cup grated Cheddar cheese
4 ounces cream cheese
    (¹/₂ an 8-ounce block), cubed
¹/₃ cup evaporated milk or whole
    milk

¹/₄ cup real grated Parmesan cheese
    (*not* the powdered kind)
¹/₂ teaspoon onion powder
¹/₂ teaspoon mustard powder
¹/₄ teaspoon salt

Preheat the oven to 350°F. Prepare the pie crust according to the package directions.

Place the remaining ingredients in a blender and process until smooth (about a minute). Pour the egg mixture into the pie crust and bake for 25 to 30 minutes, or until the middle is set and a knife inserted into the center comes out clean.

Serves 6

Chicken and Asparagus Quiche

This recipe is great for brunches as well as regular meals. I used baby asparagus (which I found at the $1 store) when testing this recipe, but you can use any type of asparagus—spears, tips, or pieces.

1 ready-made 9-inch pie crust

3 eggs

1/3 cup evaporated milk or whole milk

One 10-ounce can chunk white meat chicken, rinsed, drained, and flaked

One 15-ounce can cut asparagus that includes tips

1 cup shredded real Parmesan, Swiss, or Jack cheese

Preheat the oven to 425°F. Prepare the pie crust according to the package directions.

Whisk the eggs and milk in a medium-sized mixing bowl until combined. Add the chicken. Remove about half of the asparagus from the can (use the rest as a side dish for one or two), and stir it and the cheese in with the egg and chicken.

Pour into the pie crust and bake for about 35 minutes, or until a knife inserted into the center comes out clean.

Serves 6

Tomato and Olive Quiche

This quiche has a sort of Italian flavor to it. It makes a nice main course for dinner, in addition to being a terrific brunch dish. The nice thing is, you just mix everything together and bake. (You don't even need a pie pan if you use the ready-made crusts in tins.)

1 ready-made 9-inch pie crust

3 eggs

1/3 cup evaporated milk or whole milk (low-fat is okay)

2 teaspoons onion powder

1/2 teaspoon dried basil

1/2 teaspoon dried oregano

1/2 teaspoon garlic powder

1 cup real shredded Parmesan (*not the powdered kind*), Swiss, or Jack cheese

One 2.25-ounce can sliced black olives, drained

One 14.5-ounce can diced tomatoes, drained

Preheat the oven to 425°F. Prepare the pie crust as directed on the package.

In a medium-sized mixing bowl, whisk together the eggs and milk. When well combined, add the onion powder, basil, oregano, and garlic powder, and whisk again. Stir in the cheese, olives, and 1 scant cup of the drained tomatoes.

Pour the egg mixture into the pie crust and bake for about 35 minutes, or until a knife inserted into the center comes out clean. Just before serving, if desired, top the quiche with the remaining tomatoes.

Serves 6

Curried Pumpkin Quiche

Many people love pumpkin, yet they miss out on this tasty fruit in its savory incarnations. This quiche is simple to make and has the unmistakable taste of pumpkin, along with curry and cumin. It won't look exactly like a regular quiche; the pumpkin has a way of coloring and smoothing the top. Remember that pumpkin is loaded with vitamin A. (Try using leftover pumpkin in a milkshake with cinnamon, nutmeg, and cloves.)

1 ready-made 9-inch pie crust

3 eggs

1/2 cup evaporated milk or whole milk

3/4 cup canned pumpkin (*not* pumpkin-pie filling)

1 1/2 teaspoons curry powder

1 teaspoon onion powder

1/2 teaspoon garlic powder

1/2 teaspoon ground cumin

1/2 teaspoon ground black pepper

1/4 teaspoon salt

1 cup shredded real Parmesan cheese (*not* the powdered kind)

Preheat the oven to 425°F. Prepare the pie crust according to the package directions.

In a medium mixing bowl, combine the eggs, milk, pumpkin, curry powder, onion powder, garlic powder, cumin, pepper, and salt. Whisk until well blended, then stir in the cheese.

Pour the mixture into the pie crust and bake for about 35 minutes, or until a knife inserted into the center comes out clean.

Serves 6

Southwestern Egg Bake

This is a great dish for brunches or big breakfasts. It's also very easy.

9 eggs

1/2 cup evaporated milk or whole
milk

1 teaspoon onion powder

1/2 teaspoon garlic powder

1/2 teaspoon dried oregano

1/4 teaspoon ground cumin

1/4 teaspoon ground black pepper

1/8 teaspoon salt

2 cups shredded Cheddar cheese

One 15-ounce can corn, drained

One 15-ounce can diced tomatoes,
drained

One 4-ounce can diced chilies,
drained

One 4-ounce can sliced black olives,
drained

Preheat the oven to 325°F. Coat a 9 × 13-inch glass baking dish with oil or nonstick spray.

In a large mixing bowl, combine the eggs, milk, onion powder, garlic powder, oregano, cumin, pepper, and salt. Whisk together until well blended. Stir in the remaining ingredients, and pour into the prepared baking dish. Bake for 1 hour. The dish is ready when the edges are browned and the center is set.

Serves 8

Baked Egg Squares with Pesto, Cheese, and Artichoke

Consider serving these eggs with sourdough toast or baguettes. If you have some egg squares left over, try making a sandwich using them as you would a slice of meat. You could add roasted red peppers, *peperoncini*, and sliced olives.

Two 6-ounce jars marinated
    artichoke hearts
4 eggs
1/2 cup evaporated milk or whole
    milk
3 tablespoons prepared pesto

1/4 teaspoon dried red pepper flakes
2 cups shredded Jack cheese or
    1 cup shredded Cheddar cheese
    and 1 cup real shredded
    Parmesan cheese (*not* the powdered
    kind)

Preheat the oven to 350°F. Coat an 8 × 8-inch pan with oil or nonstick spray.

Coarsely chop the artichoke hearts. In a medium-sized mixing bowl, gently combine the eggs, milk, pesto, and red pepper flakes until the eggs are mixed (they should be more lemon-colored than gold-colored). Stir in the artichokes and cheese. Pour the mixture into the prepared pan and bake for about 30 minutes, or until the edges begin to turn golden-brown and a knife inserted into the center comes out clean.

Serves 6

Ham and Cheese Scramble

Ham from a can is excellent in eggs if you know the secret, which is to fry the ham first. So next time you want to make something a little different for a weekend brunch, this recipe will simplify your life.

1 tablespoon cooking oil or butter	**4 to 6 eggs**
One 5-ounce can ham	**1/2 cup shredded cheese**

Put the oil or butter in a frying pan and place over medium heat. Drain and dice the ham, then add it to the frying pan. Turn the ham periodically to help it "brown" evenly. That's the whole goal—the searing of the meat. When done, set aside.

After you've cooked the ham, add nonstick spray or oil to the pan if needed, then add the eggs. Stir the eggs to scramble. Before they set, add the ham and cheese, making sure the cheese has some time to melt.

Serve at once.

Serves 2 to 3

Corn, Cheese, and Potato Scramble

If you like scrambled eggs, it's fun to add other flavors and textures to them. This dish is terrific for brunch or dinner.

One 15-ounce can sliced potatoes, rinsed and drained	One 15-ounce can corn, drained
Cooking oil	6 eggs
Salt and pepper	1 cup grated Jack or Cheddar cheese

Dice the potatoes. Place about a tablespoon of oil in a frying pan over medium heat. Add the potatoes, then salt and pepper to taste. Sauté the potatoes until they are hot and beginning to turn golden-brown. Add the corn and sauté for another minute or so. Place the potatoes and corn on a plate and set aside.

Add a little more oil or nonstick spray and break the eggs into the pan. Scramble the eggs over medium-low heat. When nearly done, add the cheese and continue to scramble. When the cheese has melted, add the potatoes and corn, and sauté for another minute or so, just until hot. Don't cook the eggs too long or they may become too dry. Add more salt and pepper to taste if desired.

Serves 4

Curry-Stuffed Eggs

Hard-boiled eggs are a great snack to keep in the refrigerator for ready protein. I finally broke down and got one of those "hen" cookers, the kind you fill with water and it automatically makes the hard-boiled eggs for you. I like it a lot—it eliminates the occasional green yolks from overcooking that can happen with the saucepan method.

6 hard-boiled eggs

1/4 cup mayonnaise

1 teaspoon rice vinegar or cider vinegar

3/4 teaspoon curry powder

1/4 teaspoon onion powder

1/4 teaspoon ground cumin

1/4 teaspoon sugar

1/8 teaspoon salt

Slice the eggs lengthwise, then put the yolks in a bowl. Add the remaining ingredients (except the egg whites) to the yolks, then mash with a fork until smooth. If the egg mixture seems dry, add 1 tablespoon of water and mash again. Fill the egg whites with the egg-yolk mixture.

Makes 12 egg halves

Sauces and Dressings

CHAPTER 11

Basic Vinaigrette

A vinaigrette goes well on many salads and vegetables. And it's a good way to get some healthy oils into your diet.

**3 tablespoons olive oil or other
    cooking oil**
**2 tablespoons balsamic vinegar or
    rice vinegar**

Sugar to taste (optional)

Whisk all of the ingredients together until well blended.

Serves 2

Note: For a larger batch (about ⅔ cup), use ⅓ cup cooking oil and ¼ cup vinegar.

Lemon-Basil Vinaigrette

This dressing is excellent on many salads and vegetables with a Mediterranean flair.

$^1/_2$ cup olive oil

$^1/_4$ cup rice vinegar

1 tablespoon bottled lemon juice

$^1/_2$ teaspoon dried basil

$^1/_2$ teaspoon dried oregano

$^1/_8$ teaspoon salt

Combine all of the ingredients and mix well.

Makes about $^3/_4$ cup

Easy Raspberry Vinaigrette

Here's a simple way to whip up a nice raspberry vinaigrette, which is wonderful on mixed greens with feta cheese and toasted pecans. Use the all-fruit or spreadable fruit found in your grocer's jam and jelly section. The consistency makes for easy whisking, whereas normal jam, jelly, or preserves tend to be quite thick, especially when refrigerated. It's okay to use the no-sugar-added kind, too. In fact, I prefer it.

One 12-ounce jar (or 1 cup) raspberry
    spreadable fruit
¹/₃ cup balsamic vinegar

¹/₂ teaspoon salt (more if desired)
¹/₂ teaspoon ground black pepper
¹/₂ cup olive oil

In a small to medium mixing bowl, whisk together the spreadable fruit, vinegar, salt, and pepper until blended. While whisking, slowly add the olive oil and whisk until emulsified.

Makes 1¹/₂ cups

Cumin-Lime-Mint Dressing

This dressing has no fat, but it's delicious on green salads and even fruit salads, especially those with a tropical theme.

1/3 cup bottled lime juice

1 tablespoon dried mint

1 tablespoon sugar

1/2 teaspoon ground cumin

1/8 teaspoon salt

Combine all of the ingredients and 2 tablespoons of water and shake or blend well. Let sit for a few minutes before serving.

Makes about 1/2 cup

Ginger-Lime Dressing

This makes a good dressing for fish or Asian fare.

1/2 cup peanut oil or other cooking oil	2 teaspoons sugar
1/4 cup rice vinegar	1 teaspoon ground ginger
	1/2 teaspoon soy sauce

Whisk together all of the ingredients until the vinegar blends into the oil and the dressing begins to thicken.

Makes 3/4 cup

Grandma's Salad and Coleslaw Dressing

This is a recipe my grandma came up with while running a school cafeteria back in the days when she had to use government-issued foods. She said that for some reason, they gave her loads of honey. This is one of the creative ways in which she used it, although she made it in gallons, not cups. This dressing is terrific on Pineapple-Ham Tossed Salad (page 43), but you might also try it on coleslaw and other salads.

1 cup mayonnaise	**1/2 teaspoon garlic powder**
1/2 cup wine vinegar or rice vinegar	**1/4 teaspoon ground cumin**
1/3 cup honey	**Pinch salt**

Whisk together all of the ingredients until thoroughly blended.

Makes about 1 2/3 cups

Orange-Dill Sauce

This sauce makes a nice accompaniment for salmon or tuna steaks. If your fish is a strong-tasting one, you may want to add extra dill. You might also try this sauce on pork and chicken. Chilled, it makes an unusual and tasty salad dressing that's low in fat (if you use nonfat yogurt) and salt.

1 cup plain yogurt (nonfat is okay)   1 teaspoon dried dill
1/2 cup orange juice   1/4 teaspoon salt
1 teaspoon onion powder

Combine all of the ingredients in a small saucepan and stir over low-medium heat. It should not boil—just heat it through and stir until smooth.

Makes 1 1/2 cups

Lemon-Horseradish Sauce

This is a great sauce for seafood, and in fact, I recommend it as an accompaniment to Baked Salmon Croquettes (page 129).

1 cup mayonnaise

1/4 cup prepared horseradish

1 tablespoon plus 1 teaspoon bottled
  lemon juice

1/4 teaspoon garlic powder

1 to 2 teaspoons dried parsley or
  dried chives for color (optional)

Combine all of the ingredients in a small bowl. Stir well.

Makes 1 1/4 cups

Emergency Chicken Gravy

This has actually happened to me: I thought the crowd was the one that did *not* like gravy (yes, there are those people). I poured out the chicken drippings and served. The first "Where's the gravy?" just about made me faint. It's good to have a backup plan. By the way, you can easily double or triple this recipe. And bouillon has virtually no calories or fat.

1 chicken bouillon cube

1 tablespoon butter

2 tablespoons cornstarch dissolved
    in a little cold water

Salt and ground black pepper

Put 1 cup of water, the bouillon, and butter on to boil in a small saucepan. When boiling, add the cornstarch mixture and stir until thickened. Add salt and pepper if desired.

Makes about 1 cup

Emergency Beef Gravy

Follow the recipe above, substituting a beef bouillon cube.

Emergency Vegetarian Gravy

Follow the recipe above, substituting a vegetable bouillon cube.

Quick Seafood Sauce

Here's a super simple sauce that's terrific over rice or noodles or as a filler in lasagna.

**Two 10.5-ounce cans cream of celery
soup**
One 12-ounce can evaporated milk
(nonfat is okay)

Two 6-ounce cans crab, drained
**One 6-ounce can tiny or broken
shrimp, drained**

Whisk together the soup and milk. Stir in the crab and shrimp. Heat and serve.

Makes about 5 cups

Seafood Cocktail Sauce

This is a great sauce to make ahead of time, as chilling it in the refrigerator only enhances its flavor. Use it for seafood such as shrimp, crab, or oysters.

1 cup ketchup

2 tablespoons prepared horseradish

1 teaspoon balsamic vinegar

1 teaspoon Worcestershire sauce

1/2 teaspoon onion powder

1/8 teaspoon salt

1/8 teaspoon sugar

Pinch cayenne or hot pepper sauce

(optional)

In a small mixing bowl, whisk together all of the ingredients. Chill for 1 hour or more in the refrigerator before serving.

Makes 1 cup

Pesto Mayonnaise

This is a great dressing for sandwiches, artichokes, and seafood. Try it on an Italian sandwich with provolone, roasted red peppers (from a jar), and salami. Or cut up artichoke bottoms (from a can) and use it as a dip.

Mayonnaise   **Prepared pesto sauce**

For each ¼ cup of mayonnaise, stir in 1 teaspoon of prepared pesto sauce.

Spicy Tomato-Cheese Sauce

This sauce is terrific over a number of pasta dishes. Try it with tortellini, ravioli, rigatoni, and stuffed shells.

One 28-ounce can tomato puree

One 28-ounce can diced tomatoes

2 teaspoons sugar

1 teaspoon garlic powder

1 teaspoon dried basil

1 teaspoon salt (optional)

1 teaspoon dried red pepper flakes
   (or 1/2 teaspoon cayenne)

1/2 teaspoon onion powder

1/2 teaspoon dried oregano

2 cups shredded Cheddar cheese

1 cup real shredded Parmesan cheese
   (*not* the powdered kind)

Canned sliced black olives or sliced
   mushrooms (optional)

In a medium saucepan, combine all of the ingredients and cook over medium heat, stirring periodically. The sauce is ready when it's good and hot and the cheese has almost completely melted.

Serves 8

Tomato and Walnut Pasta Sauce

Serve this sauce over fettuccine, linguine, tagliatelle, or even egg noodles. Take care not to use aluminum cookware, as it may react to the acids in the tomatoes.

One 28-ounce can whole peeled tomatoes, *not* drained

One 15-ounce can onions, *not* drained

1/4 cup white wine or 1 tablespoon rice vinegar plus 3 tablespoons water

1 teaspoon balsamic vinegar

1 teaspoon dried basil

1/2 teaspoon salt

1/2 teaspoon dried rosemary leaves

1/2 teaspoon garlic powder

3 tablespoons cornstarch dissolved in a little cold water

1 cup real grated Parmesan cheese (*not* the powdered kind), plus extra for the table

1 tablespoon cooking oil (such as olive oil)

1 cup chopped walnuts

Pour the juice from the tomato can into a medium-sized saucepan. Coarsely chop the tomatoes and add them to the juice. Add the onions with liquid, wine or rice vinegar, balsamic vinegar, basil, salt, rosemary, garlic powder, and cornstarch mixture to the saucepan, and bring to a boil. Add the Parmesan cheese and stir. Continue heating while the sauce thickens, about 5 minutes. You may let it simmer longer while you prepare other things, if desired.

Shortly before serving time, pour the cooking oil into a small pan and add the walnuts, stirring to coat. Cook over low-medium heat for about 5 minutes, stirring to keep nuts from burning. Serve the sautéed walnuts on top of or mixed into the tomato mixture.

Serves 8

Roasted Red Pepper and Zucchini Sauce

Roasted red peppers impart an unusual flavor to red pasta sauce. Use this sauce for regular pastas or on filled pastas such as tortellini or ravioli. Be sure not to use an aluminum saucepan, as it may react with the tomato sauce and peppers.

One 12-ounce jar roasted red
    peppers, drained
One 8-ounce can tomato sauce
One 14.5-ounce can chicken broth
One 14.5-ounce can zucchini in
    Italian tomato sauce
1 teaspoon sugar

$1/2$ teaspoon salt
$1/2$ teaspoon dried thyme
$1/4$ teaspoon garlic powder
$1/4$ teaspoon onion powder
$1/4$ teaspoon ground black pepper
1 cup shredded real Parmesan
    cheese

Puree the roasted red peppers. The puree should be a little chunky.

Combine the puree with the tomato sauce, chicken broth, zucchini, sugar, salt, thyme, garlic powder, onion powder, and black pepper in a saucepan. Stir to combine, then add Parmesan cheese. Bring the mixture to a low boil and cook until the sauce is good and hot. Serve over pasta or eggplant.

Makes about 6 cups

Homemade Barbecue Sauce

Here's a quick version of barbecue sauce that is really enhanced with the use of Liquid Smoke®, found near ketchup and barbecue sauces in your grocery store. Brush this sauce on during the last few minutes of grilling. It also makes great barbecued beans or tuna sandwiches (page 137).

2¹/₂ cups ketchup	1 teaspoon onion powder
¹/₂ cup prepared mustard	¹/₂ teaspoon salt
¹/₄ cup pancake syrup or molasses	¹/₂ teaspoon cayenne
¹/₄ cup brown sugar	1¹/₂ teaspoons Liquid Smoke®
1 teaspoon garlic powder	(optional)

To make Homemade Barbecue Sauce, simply combine all ingredients and stir until blended.

Makes about 3 cups

Pizza Sauce

This recipe can easily be doubled.

One 8-ounce can tomato sauce   **¹/₄ teaspoon garlic powder**
¹/₂ teaspoon sugar   **¹/₄ teaspoon onion powder**
¹/₂ teaspoon dried basil

Combine all of the ingredients until blended.

Makes about 1 cup (enough for one pizza)

Enchilada Sauce

This is a lifesaver when you need enchilada sauce and don't have it on hand. Use it for enchiladas, burritos, or anywhere a Mexican sauce would be useful.

One 15-ounce can tomato sauce

1 teaspoon sugar

1/2 teaspoon garlic powder

1/2 teaspoon onion powder

1/2 teaspoon chili powder

1/4 teaspoon ground cumin

1/8 to 1/4 teaspoon cayenne (optional)

Combine all of the ingredients. The sauce may be heated before serving or it may be used at room temperature, right after it's been made.

Makes about 1 3/4 cups

Caramel Syrup

This is a syrup my grandma used to make. Many people used to make their own syrups, but since we can buy pancake syrup easily enough nowadays, we don't anymore. However, caramel syrup (without preservatives) is wonderful in many recipes. You can make up a batch and keep it in a sealed glass container and it will last quite a while in the refrigerator. Try it with cakes, pies, sweet potatoes, ice cream, pancakes, waffles, and milk.

1 cup light corn syrup
2 cups firmly packed light brown
   sugar

1 teaspoon vanilla extract
1/2 to 3/4 teaspoon liquid butter
   flavoring

Put 1 cup of water, the syrup, and the sugar in a medium saucepan over high heat. Stir frequently and bring to a boil. Once boiling, quickly remove from the heat and reduce the heat to medium. Put the saucepan back on over medium heat and cook for 15 minutes, stirring frequently. Remove from the heat and add the vanilla and 1/2 teaspoon butter flavoring, stirring well. If a stronger butter flavor is desired, stir in an additional 1/4 teaspoon butter flavoring.

When cool, cover and store in the refrigerator. See Note.

Makes 2 cups

Note: Like most syrups, this one will store nearly indefinitely if refrigerated in a sealed container.

Chocolate Dipping Sauce
or Syrup

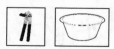

If you've ever stood watch over chocolate in a double-boiler, I think you're going to like the simplicity of this sauce. Just throw the chocolate into the microwave—no fuss, no burning, no time. Use this as a dipping sauce to coat different foods, or as a syrup.

½ cup semisweet chocolate chips   **1 tablespoon cooking oil**

Place the chocolate chips in a small microwave-safe bowl. Pour the cooking oil over the chocolate chips (this not only helps the dipping consistency, it also gives the chocolate a nice sheen). Microwave at full power for 45 seconds. Stir the chocolate, then heat another 15 seconds. When you stir again, the chocolate should be melted. If it hasn't melted completely, heat it for another 10 seconds. Repeat if necessary.

When thoroughly melted, you may use the sauce over ice cream and cake, or you may dip foods of your choice: strawberries, bananas, brandy-soaked maraschino cherries (see page 277), pretzels, etc. You might also try cookies. Even store-bought cookies seem special if they're dipped or half-dipped in chocolate. Or try the Easy Coconut Macaroons on page 283.

Makes ½ cup

Note: Chocolate hardens faster if foods are cold, but it's not necessary. However, you should place the dipped items in the refrigerator until ready to eat, as this will harden the chocolate faster and keep it firm. (Chocolate will need about 1/2 hour in the refrigerator to harden.) Also, don't let the chocolate get too warm or it will begin to melt.

Ginger-Peach Sauce

Here's a sauce that's a breeze to make. Drizzle it on ice cream or cake, or serve it with pork, poultry, or Asian-themed meals. It would probably make a nice dipping sauce, too.

One 15-ounce can peaches, sliced or halved, drained

1/4 to 1/2 teaspoon ground ginger

1/2 teaspoon bottled lemon juice

Puree the peaches with a hand blender or in a regular blender. Add 1/4 teaspoon of ginger and lemon juice, puree again, and taste. (Some people prefer more ginger, while others prefer it mild; season to your taste.) If you find the ginger overpowering, stir in more lemon juice.

Makes 1 cup

Orange-Spiced Cranberry Sauce

During holiday-time crunches, it's nice to know there are some side dishes you can make easily and even prepare ahead of time. This is a tasty alternative to standard holiday cranberry sauce. There's no cooking involved, it takes only minutes, and it even has real oranges in it (in the marmalade).

One 16-ounce can whole-berry cranberry sauce

3/4 cup orange marmalade (easier to stir if at room temperature)

1 teaspoon bottled lime juice

1/2 teaspoon ground cinnamon

1/4 teaspoon ground cloves

1/4 teaspoon ground ginger

1/2 cup chopped walnuts (optional)

Empty the cranberry sauce into a medium-sized mixing bowl. If the marmalade is cold, let it sit out for an hour or heat it in the microwave for about 10 to 15 seconds on high. Combine all of the ingredients in the bowl, stirring until well mixed. Serve immediately, or chill in the refrigerator for later.

Makes 2 cups

Minted Yogurt Sauce

This sauce is a great addition to falafel (page 197), samosas (page 166), and several other Middle Eastern–type dishes.

1 cup plain yogurt

1 tablespoon dried mint

1/2 teaspoon bottled lemon or lime
    juice

1/4 teaspoon garlic powder

1/4 teaspoon ground cumin

1/4 teaspoon sugar

Pinch salt

Combine all of the ingredients and mix well. Chill if the sauce will not be served right away.

Makes 1 cup

Desserts

CHAPTER 12

Apple Upside-Down Cake

I love apples in just about any incarnation. If you prefer to use fresh apples, feel free, but these canned apples work beautifully. Plus, you can store them indefinitely and make the cake whenever you want. Use either round or square cake pans, whichever you prefer.

4 tablespoons (½ stick) **butter, melted**

1 cup packed brown sugar

2 teaspoons ground cinnamon

One 15-ounce can apples

1 tablespoon bottled lemon juice

½ cup raisins

½ cup chopped walnuts

1 box white cake mix

1¼ cups apple juice (or an amount equal to the amount of water called for in the cake package instructions)

¼ cup cooking oil (or the amount called for in the cake package instructions)

2 eggs (or the amount called for in the cake package directions)

Preheat the oven to 350°F. Pour the melted butter equally between two 9-inch cake pans (2 tablespoons each) and tip to coat. Mix the brown sugar with the cinnamon and sprinkle half over the butter in each cake pan. Drain the apples, reserving 2 tablespoons of juice. Sprinkle 1 tablespoon of juice into each pan, stirring to mix a little.

Dice the apples, then put them in a small bowl and drizzle with the lemon juice. Toss to coat, then put half of the apples in one pan, half in the other. Sprinkle the raisins (¼ cup in each pan), and then the walnuts (¼ cup in each pan), on top of the apples.

Prepare the cake mix according to the package directions, substituting apple juice for the water called for on the cake box. Divide the batter evenly between the two pans. Use a spatula to smooth the surfaces if needed. Bake for about 35 minutes, or until a knife inserted into the centers comes out clean. Let the cakes cool for about 15 minutes before inverting onto plates.

Serves 12

Note: You may use 8-inch cake pans instead of the 9-inch. Just keep in mind that they'll probably require a couple more minutes of baking time.

French Apple Cheesecake

This recipe starts off as a very basic (yet tasty) cheesecake and becomes special by adding apple-pie filling and graham cracker crumbs. These simple additions make it a nice dessert for guests. (And it's easily doubled.)

Two 8-ounce packages cream cheese, at room temperature

1/2 cup sugar

3/4 teaspoon vanilla extract

2 eggs

1 ready-to-use 9-inch graham cracker pie crust (or see recipe on page 160)

One 20-ounce can apple-pie filling

1 tablespoon melted butter

1/4 cup graham cracker crumbs

Preheat the oven to 350°F. If the cream cheese isn't at room temperature, unwrap each package and heat it in the microwave for about 15 seconds. Check the cream cheese. If it's still cold and hard, heat it again in 10-second intervals until it's softer.

Mix the cream cheese, sugar, and vanilla in a medium-sized mixing bowl until smooth. Add the eggs and blend well. Pour the mixture into the crust. Bake for about 40 minutes, or until the middle is almost set. Remove from the oven and let cool. Chill in the refrigerator for at least 3 hours. (You may use the freezer to help speed things along, but you'll need to keep a watch so it doesn't freeze. Try 1 hour.)

When ready to serve, place apple-pie filling pieces on top of the cheesecake along with their syrup. You can arrange them decoratively if you wish. You will probably use only about half the can; use the rest for an ice-cream topping or a second cheesecake.

Melt the butter, then stir it into the graham cracker crumbs. It should make lots of different-sized crumbs. Sprinkle them over the top of the apples.

Serves 6 to 8

Mango Chutney Cheesecake

Try something new with traditional cheesecake by using mango chutney as a topping. Chutney is a wonderful Indian condiment full of sweet, sour, and spicy flavors. Just make sure you choose a chutney that is on the sweeter side, rather than the savory. I find Trader Joe's brand of Major Grey's Mango Chutney works very well for this. Also, you may use Neufchatel or low-fat cream cheese to trim calories.

Two 8-ounce packages cream cheese, softened

1/2 cup sugar

3/4 teaspoon vanilla extract

2 eggs

One ready-to-use graham cracker pie crust (or see recipe on page 160)

One 8-ounce jar Major Grey's Mango Chutney

Preheat oven to 350°F. In a medium mixing bowl, beat the cream cheese, sugar, and vanilla together until smooth. Add the eggs and beat until the entire mixture is well blended. Pour the batter into the pie crust and bake for about 40 minutes, until the middle is nearly set.

Cool and refrigerate for about three hours, or even overnight (see Note). When ready to serve, spread the mango chutney onto the cheesecake to cover. Or, you may slice individual servings of cheesecake and top with spoonfuls of chutney. (One of my testers preferred the look of the dessert the latter way.)

Serves 6 to 8

Note: If you're in a hurry, you can put the cheesecake in the freezer for about 1 hour.

Apple-Raisin Bread Pudding

This is an easy version of a fairly easy recipe, but in comfort-food points, it scores very high. Because of its simplicity, it makes an ideal holiday treat as well. I use nonfat evaporated milk to cut calories, and it tastes just great.

4 to 6 slices raisin bread or white bread

3 to 5 tablespoons raisins

One 15-ounce can sliced apples, drained (or two sliced, peeled apples)

1/4 cup chopped walnuts

3 eggs

One 12-ounce can evaporated milk

1/2 cup apple cider or apple juice

2/3 cup plus 2 tablespoons brown sugar

1 1/2 teaspoons ground cinnamon

1/2 teaspoon ground nutmeg

Preheat the oven to 325°F. Lightly coat an 8 × 8-inch baking dish or pan with oil or nonstick spray.

Lightly toast the bread (and I mean just barely, so that it's more like dried bread than toast). Slice each piece diagonally into four triangles. Lay about eight bread triangles in your dish, or enough to cover the bottom loosely. If you're not using raisin bread, add 2 tablespoons of raisins to the top of the bread layer.

Slice the apple pieces so that they're about 1/4 inch thick each. Lay about half the apples on top of the bread (and raisins). Lay another eight bread triangles on top of the apples. Sprinkle

3 tablespoons raisins and ¼ cup of chopped walnuts on the bread layer. Lay the remaining apples on top of the raisins and walnuts (it doesn't matter if you lay them decoratively, as they'll move around with the egg batter).

In a medium mixing bowl, whisk together the eggs, milk, and apple cider or juice until blended. In a small bowl, whisk together ⅔ cup of brown sugar with the cinnamon and nutmeg. (It's easier to stir into the eggs that way.) Whisk the brown-sugar mix into the egg batter, then pour over the bread and apple slices. Push down on the bread so that everything is moist. Sprinkle the remaining 2 tablespoons of brown sugar over the top. (I use my hands to do this, as the brown sugar is hard to sprinkle evenly.)

Bake, uncovered, for about 60 minutes, or until a knife inserted into the center comes out clean.

Serves 6

Sour Cream–Banana Cake with Milk Chocolate Frosting

This cake is pretty simple—just toss all the dry ingredients into a bowl, then beat in the moist ingredients. And you can honestly say it's made from "scratch." The frosting below also uses some sour cream, so make sure you have enough for both (one 16-ounce container is more than enough).

2¹/2 cups all-purpose flour	3/4 cup sour cream
1¹/2 cups sugar	2 eggs
1¹/2 teaspoons baking powder	2 teaspoons banana extract or
1 teaspoon baking soda	flavoring
1 teaspoon salt	1 teaspoon vanilla extract or
¹/2 cup (1 stick) butter, softened	flavoring
(see Notes)	Milk Chocolate Frosting (recipe
Three 4-ounce jars banana baby food	follows)

Preheat the oven to 350°F. Oil and lightly flour two 9-inch cake pans or one 9 × 13-inch pan.

Put the flour, sugar, baking powder, baking soda, and salt in a large mixing bowl and stir to blend. Add the softened butter, baby food, sour cream, eggs, banana extract, and vanilla extract, and beat until smooth. The batter will be a little stiff.

If you're using two round cake pans, pour equal amounts of batter into each pan, then bake for about 25 minutes, or until a knife inserted in the centers comes out clean. For the 9 × 13-inch pan, pour in the batter and bake for about 35 minutes, or until a knife inserted in the center comes out clean. Let the cake(s) cool before frosting.

Notes: You may use 8-inch cake pans. Just note that they may require a few more minutes of cooking time.

To soften butter, let it sit out for an hour or heat it in a microwave on high for 10 to 15 seconds. If necessary, heat it again in 5-second increments.

Milk Chocolate Frosting

1 cup milk-chocolate chips (half a
   12-ounce package)
1/4 cup (1/2 stick) butter
1/2 cup sour cream

1 teaspoon vanilla extract
2 cups (one 16-ounce box)
   confectioners' sugar

Melt the chocolate chips and butter over low-medium heat in a saucepan. Let cool for about 10 minutes to stiffen. Add the sour cream, vanilla, and sugar, and stir until smooth.

Frosts one two-tiered 8-inch or 9-inch round cake,
or one 9 × 13-inch cake

Blueberry Pineapple Pie

This is an easy pie that involves more chilling than baking. (You only have to bake the crust before you begin.) Delicious with canned cherries, too!

One deep dish 9-inch pie shell, baked

One 15-ounce can blueberries

One 15-ounce can crushed pineapple

One 8-ounce bar cream cheese, softened (see Note)

7 tablespoons sugar, divided

1/2 teaspoon vanilla

1/4 teaspoon salt

1/4 cup cornstarch dissolved in a little cold water

Whipped topping for serving, if desired

Bake the pie shell according to package directions, then let it cool. Drain the juice from the blueberries and pineapple into a measuring cup to get 1 cup liquid. (Press on the pineapple with the lid and you'll get more juice.) Add water to make up anything short of the 1 cup, if needed.

Beat the cream cheese with 3 tablespoons sugar and the vanilla. Spread it along the bottom of the cooled pie crust, then chill. (Fifteen minutes in the freezer works well.)

In a medium saucepan, combine the juices with the 4 remaining tablespoons of sugar and the salt, and bring to a boil, stirring frequently. When boiling, add the cornstarch and stir a couple minutes more until thickened. Remove from the heat. Stir in the blueberries and pineapple. Let cool a few minutes, then pour over the cream cheese layer of the pie. Chill until firm (about 25 minutes in the freezer).

Serve with whipped topping, if desired.

Serves 8

Note: To speed softening, heat one bar of cream cheese, unwrapped, in the microwave 15 seconds. Check, and repeat with 10-second intervals if needed.

Caramel Cream Pie

Surprisingly easy, this was another one of my grandma's creations, and one of my grandpa's favorites. If you've never made a meringue before, don't let the prospect scare you off. It's very simple.

One 9-inch pie crust (page 157 or store-bought)

3 eggs

One 12-ounce can evaporated milk

3/4 cup Caramel Syrup (page 253) or store-bought caramel syrup or caramel ice cream topping

3 tablespoons cornstarch dissolved in a little cold water

2 tablespoons sugar

1 teaspoon vanilla extract

Bake the pie crust according to the package directions for a one-crust pie and set aside.

Preheat the oven to 400°F. Separate the eggs and set aside (I put them in coffee cups). In a medium-sized saucepan, whisk together the milk, caramel syrup, and dissolved cornstarch. When well blended, lightly beat the egg yolks, add them to the milk mixture, and stir well. Cook the mixture over medium-high heat until it boils and thickens into a puddinglike texture, stirring often. Remove from the heat and set aside while preparing the meringue topping.

Beat the egg whites until foamy and thickened. Add 1 tablespoon of sugar and continue beating until the sugar is fully blended. Add the second tablespoon of sugar and the vanilla, and continue beating until stiff peaks form.

Pour the prepared caramel filling into the precooked pie crust. Spread the meringue evenly over the top. Bake for 6 to 8 minutes, or until the meringue is golden-brown. Watch the pie carefully so the meringue doesn't burn. Chill in the refrigerator (about 3 hours) and serve cold.

Serves 6

Caramel Pecan Pie

Pecan pie is always a treat, but add caramel and it's even more special.

2 tablespoons butter, melted	3 eggs
1 cup Caramel Syrup (page 253) or store-bought caramel syrup or caramel ice cream topping	1 teaspoon vanilla extract
	1 cup pecan halves
	One unbaked 9-inch pie crust

Preheat the oven to 375°F.

In a medium-sized mixing bowl, combine the butter, caramel syrup, eggs, 2 tablespoons of water, and the vanilla extract, blending well. Stir in the pecans, which will float to the top.

Pour the mixture into the unbaked pie crust. Bake on the next-to-lowest oven rack for 45 minutes or until set in the center.

Note: The edges of the pie crust tend to cook faster than the pie filling. To avoid burning the outer crust, use pie rings or wrap aluminum foil around the edges for the first 15 minutes of baking time.

Serves 6

Old-Fashioned Cherry Cobbler

Cherry cobbler is a fairly easy dessert, but it becomes even simpler when you don't have to make the biscuit topping. Some people use canned cherry-pie filling; I prefer to use just the cherries and their syrup, since I know exactly what's going into it. With the cherry syrup in the can, you don't even need to add sugar.

Two 15-ounce cans dark pitted
sweet **bing cherries in heavy**
syrup
3 tablespoons cornstarch mixed with
a little cold water

1 can refrigerated ready-to-bake
biscuits (8 to 10 per can)
1/4 teaspoon ground cinnamon
(optional)
2 teaspoons sugar (optional)

Preheat the oven to 400°F. Coat an 8 × 8-inch pan or baking dish with nonstick spray or a little cooking oil.

In a medium saucepan, combine the cherries with their syrup and the dissolved cornstarch. Bring the mixture to a boil, stirring gently just to keep the cherries from sticking to the pan. After about 3 minutes or so of boiling, the mixture should be thickened. It's ready when the cherry syrup begins to coat the spoon.

Pour the cherries into the prepared baking dish. Separate the biscuits and place them on top of the cherries in rows. If desired, mix the cinnamon and sugar, then sprinkle over the tops of the biscuits.

Bake for 12 to 15 minutes, until the biscuits have risen and turned golden-brown.

Serves 4 to 6

Chocolate-Cherry Cordials

These cordials make elegant treats, especially around the holidays. Serve them with ice cream, with cake (instead of ice cream), or alone with a coffee drink. However, please note that they are an adult dessert, as the brandy remains at full strength.

Also, don't let the directions scare you off. It actually takes much more time to describe the process than to do it. This treat becomes an embarrassingly easy one if you use purchased chocolate sauce, eliminating the chocolate-melting step, which takes the most time and runs the risk of ruining the chocolate (see Notes). This recipe is easily doubled, tripled, etc., if you wish to make larger batches.

12 maraschino cherries (with stems if possible), **drained**
¼ cup brandy

¼ cup chocolate "instant shell"–type ice cream syrup or see recipe for Chocolate Dipping Sauce, page 254

Place the cherries in a small bowl and cover them with the brandy. Place them in the freezer for about 40 minutes. You want them firm but not frozen.

Remove the cherries from the freezer and drain the brandy. (You may want to use it for a coffee drink or an adult "Shirley Temple"–type cola drink.)

Dry the cherries with paper towels, blotting gently. If they're wet, they'll be slippery, and it will be harder to make the chocolate stick. Place a piece of waxed paper on a plate to receive the dipped cherries.

If using store-bought "instant shell" syrup, shake the chocolate syrup according to the label instructions first. If the cherries don't have stems, use a toothpick, or simply pour the chocolate in the bowl and drop the cherries into the chocolate, fishing them out gently with a fork. Place them on the waxed paper. Do not put all the cherries in at once, because cold makes the chocolate harden immediately.

If the cherries have stems, use a small bowl or cup to catch the chocolate drippings. Hold a cherry over the bowl and squeeze chocolate over it until it's covered. Place the dipped cherry on waxed paper. As you begin to accumulate more chocolate in the bowl, you may roll the cherries around in it. (It's just easier to pour the chocolate over the cherries.)

After you've dipped all the cherries, much of the chocolate will have hardened. Store the cherries in the refrigerator to ensure that they stay firm.

Makes 12 cherries

Note: Keep in mind that the cherry cordials must remain in the refrigerator if you use the "instant-shell"–type syrup, as the chocolate will melt if not kept cold. If you use homemade sauce, it can remain out of the refrigerator.

Chocolate-Raspberry Pie

Here's an easy pie that's always a crowd pleaser. Consider serving it with whipped cream. If you whip the cream yourself, try flavoring it with a little vanilla or brandy.

One ready-made 9-inch pie crust	**$1/2$ teaspoon salt**
$1/2$ cup raspberry jam	**2 eggs, beaten**
1 cup sugar	**$1/2$ cup (1 stick) unsalted butter, melted**
$1/4$ cup all-purpose flour	**1 cup semisweet chocolate chips**

Preheat the oven to 350°F. Thaw or prepare the pie crust according to the package directions. Melt the jam, and let it cool while you assemble the pie.

In a medium-sized mixing bowl, combine the sugar, flour, and salt with a fork to sift. Add the eggs and stir. Add the butter and melted jam, and stir. Stir in the chocolate chips, then pour into the pie crust.

Bake on a cookie sheet (to prevent oven spillage) for 45 minutes, or until the top has firmed. Let cool before serving. You may also serve it chilled.

Serves 6 to 8

Coconut Cake with Brown Sugar Frosting

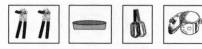

2 cups all-purpose flour (plus extra for
   dusting pans)

2¹/₂ teaspoons baking powder

³/₄ teaspoon salt

1³/₄ cups sweetened coconut flakes

¹/₂ cup (1 stick) butter

1 cup sugar

2 eggs

1¹/₂ teaspoons vanilla extract

One 13.5-ounce can coconut milk

Brown Sugar Frosting (recipe follows)

Preheat the oven to 375°F. Lightly coat two 8-inch or 9-inch cake pans or one 9 × 13-inch pan with oil, then dust them lightly with flour.

Mix the flour, baking powder, salt, and coconut flakes in a bowl, whisking to blend. In another bowl, beat the butter. (If butter is cold and hard, heat it in the microwave for about 10 to 15 seconds first.) When the butter is fluffy, beat in the sugar, eggs, and vanilla. Alternately add coconut milk and flour mixture to the butter mixture until blended.

Pour the batter into the cake pan(s) and bake for 30 to 35 minutes. The cake is done when a knife inserted into the center comes out clean. Let cool, then remove from pan(s) and frost with Brown Sugar Frosting.

Note: If you use two 8-inch pans or a 9 × 13-inch pan, you'll need a few more minutes baking time.

Brown Sugar Frosting

¹/2 cup (1 stick) butter

1 cup packed brown sugar

¹/4 cup evaporated milk or whole milk

3 cups confectioners' sugar

Melt the butter in a saucepan, then add the brown sugar. Stir over medium-high heat, blending the sugar and butter, and bring to a boil. When you're getting large bubbles and the butter is frothy, remove from the heat. Beat in the milk and sugar. Beat by hand until smooth and of a frosting consistency.

Makes enough to ice two 8-inch or 9-inch cakes
or one 9 × 13-inch cake

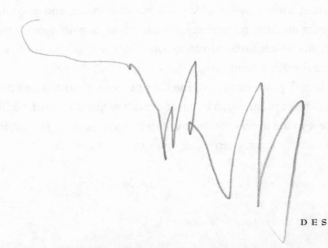

Coconut Custard

Custards can be tricky when using eggs as a thickener, because there's the very real danger of curdling. So I developed this one using cornstarch only. I found the coconut milk just a little too mild for a dessert; adding a little coconut extract does the trick. This recipe is easily doubled.

One 14-ounce can coconut milk
3 tablespoons plus 1 teaspoon
    cornstarch

$1/3$ cup sugar
$1/8$ teaspoon ground nutmeg
1 teaspoon coconut extract

Pour the coconut milk into a small saucepan, then whisk in the cornstarch, making sure the cornstarch is completely dissolved. Add the sugar, nutmeg, and coconut extract. Stir and cook over medium heat until the mixture reaches a low boil. Stir for about 5 minutes, until the mixture is thick. Make sure to continue stirring during the cooking process—it's a good job for an older child if you've got willing hands.

Once thickened, pour the custard into heatproof container(s) and cover with plastic wrap. To eliminate "skin," place plastic wrap in direct contact with the custard. Chill for several hours before serving. (I place it in the freezer for an hour first to speed cooling.) Consider serving with fruit, such as canned mandarin oranges, cherries, or pineapple, as a garnish.

Serves 3

Easy Coconut Macaroons

I don't know how long I had a package of dried coconut in my cupboard, but I finally figured out a way to use it. That and the sweetened condensed milk. These cookies have a crispy outside and a soft center. Try serving them with chocolate ice cream or a nice hot latte (or both).

4 egg whites

One 14-ounce can sweetened
   condensed milk (not
   evaporated milk)

1 1/2 teaspoons vanilla or almond
   extract

1/3 cup all-purpose flour

1/4 teaspoon salt

One 14-ounce package sweetened
   flaked coconut

Preheat the oven to 350°F. Coat a cookie sheet very well with oil or nonstick spray (these cookies are a little sticky).

In a large mixing bowl, whisk the egg whites with a fork for several seconds, until they begin to be a little frothy. Stir in the condensed milk and vanilla or almond extract, mixing well. In a small bowl, mix the flour with the salt, then stir it into the milk mixture. Add the coconut and blend together.

Drop by spoonfuls onto the cookie sheet about 2 inches apart (the cookies should be around

2 inches in diameter). Bake for 12 to 15 minutes, until the edges and tops have browned—almost like hash-brown potatoes.

Makes about 36 cookies

VARIATION

Chocolate-Dipped Coconut Macaroons

Follow the recipe above, and dip them in Chocolate Dipping Sauce (page 254). You can coat them completely or dip just half of each cookie.

Cranberry Pie

I think I've just learned where the saying "easy as pie" came from. This one's a snap. And it's perfect as a new twist on holiday desserts, especially for those wanting something a little less sweet. Drizzle it with chocolate syrup at serving time for extra flair.

One frozen 9-inch pie crust
One 16-ounce can whole-berry
    cranberry sauce
1/2 cup sugar

1 tablespoon melted butter
3 tablespoons cornstarch dissolved
    in a little cold water

Preheat the oven to 375°F. Prepare the pie crust according to the package directions. Pierce it with fork tines in several spots and bake it for 5 minutes before adding the filling.

Mash the cranberry sauce with a fork. Stir in the sugar, melted butter, and dissolved cornstarch. Pour into the prepared pie crust.

Bake for 35 to 40 minutes, or until the middle is set.

Serves 6 to 8

Note: I don't recommend substituting flour for cornstarch in this recipe, because the acid in the cranberries could make the flour less effective.

Cranberry Sorbet

Consider serving this sorbet around the holidays for a refreshing change of pace from the usual desserts. It's great for people who are watching their fat intake (there's virtually none in this dessert) and their sodium. Just remember that the cranberry sauce must be frozen for at least 18 hours before you make the dessert.

One 15-ounce can whole-berry cranberry sauce, frozen for at least 18 hours

1 to 2 teaspoons bottled lemon or lime juice

When you're ready to make the sorbet, run the can under hot water (or submerge) for 1 to 2 minutes. Open the can and pour any liquid into the container you'll use to process the fruit. Slice the frozen cranberry sauce into chunks, or simply pull out chunks with a fork, and combine them with the rest in the container to process. Add 1 teaspoon of bottled lemon or lime juice, 2 if you like it more tart. Puree with hand blender, blender, or food processor until smooth.

Cranberry sauce has a different consistency than other fruits—something more like a gelato. You may want to freeze it again for 30 minutes before serving (you can freeze it up to 8 hours before serving).

Serves 3

Low-Fat Brownies

Many people don't realize that you can substitute pureed fruits for all or some of the fat called for in many baking recipes. This recipe uses pureed apples (applesauce) but canned pumpkin (pumpkin puree) or 1 jar of baby-food bananas, carrots, or plums works quite well, too. You may also drain canned pears, peaches, plums, etc., puree them, and then use them as fat substitutes. You may note a small difference in the consistency of the brownies—more cakelike and less crumbly (which I actually prefer)—but the chocolate flavor is all there! By the way, I don't recommend doubling this recipe because it takes forever for the center to set and it can dry the edges.

³/₄ cup all-purpose flour

¹/₄ cup plus 2 tablespoons cocoa
  powder

1 cup sugar

¹/₃ cup applesauce

2 eggs

1 teaspoon vanilla extract

¹/₄ cup chopped walnuts, pecans, or
  almonds (optional)

Preheat oven to 325°F. Lightly coat an 8 × 8-inch baking pan with oil or nonstick spray. In a medium mixing bowl, whisk together flour and cocoa powder. Stir in sugar, then stir in remaining ingredients until well blended. Pour batter into prepared pan and spread evenly. Bake about 25 minutes, or until edges pull away from the sides of the pan and the middle is almost set. (The key is not to overbake or dry out the brownies, which is more of a risk without the traditional fat.)

Serves 9

Peanut Butter Fudge

Just right for those chocolate–peanut butter cravings. This is something that's easy for kids to make. (And it's a great time-saver for holiday baking.)

16 ounces semisweet chocolate chips (roughly one-and-a-half 12-ounce packages, or about 3 cups' worth)

One 14-ounce can sweetened condensed milk (not evaporated milk)

1/2 cup peanut butter (any kind but "natural" style)

1 cup chopped nuts (optional)

2 teaspoons vanilla extract

Coat an 8 × 8-inch square pan with oil or nonstick spray.

Combine the chocolate, condensed milk, peanut butter, and nuts, if desired, in a medium-sized microwave-proof mixing bowl. Microwave on high for about 2 minutes. (You may also melt the chocolate mixture in a saucepan over low heat if you prefer.) After 2 minutes in the microwave, stir the chocolate mixture. If it hasn't completely melted, heat it a little longer until melted (try 10-second intervals). When everything is melted and combined, stir in the vanilla.

Turn the fudge into your pan and smooth it over. Cover and put the pan in the refrigerator to chill. After about an hour it will be cooled enough to cut into squares.

Makes sixty-four 1-inch squares

Sweet Potato Cake

Sweet potatoes are loaded with vitamin A. This cake tastes a lot like carrot cake or pumpkin bread. You may want to frost it with Cream Cheese Frosting (recipe follows) or enjoy it just as it is.

2 cups all-purpose flour	1/2 teaspoon ground cloves
2 cups sugar	One 15-ounce can sweet potatoes
1 teaspoon baking powder	1 cup cooking oil
1 teaspoon salt	4 eggs
1 teaspoon baking soda	1 cup chopped nuts or raisins
1 teaspoon ground cinnamon	(optional)
1/2 teaspoon ground nutmeg	Cream Cheese Frosting (recipe follows)

Preheat the oven to 325°F. Coat a 9 × 13-inch pan with oil, then dust it lightly with flour.

In a medium-sized mixing bowl, combine the flour, sugar, baking powder, salt, baking soda, cinnamon, nutmeg, and cloves. Stir with a whisk or fork until evenly distributed.

Drain the sweet potatoes, reserving 1/4 cup of the syrup. Mash or puree the sweet potatoes with the 1/4 cup of syrup. Add the mashed sweet potatoes, oil, eggs, and nuts or raisins to the flour mixture. Beat until smooth.

Pour the batter into the prepared pan and bake for about 40 minutes, or until a knife inserted in the center comes out clean. Cool before frosting, if desired.

Serves 12

Cream Cheese Frosting

8 ounces cream cheese, softened   1 teaspoon vanilla extract
1 cup confectioners' sugar

If the cream cheese is not at room temperature, remove the wrapping and heat it in the microwave oven for about 15 seconds.

Beat the cream cheese, sugar, and vanilla until they attain a smooth, frostinglike consistency.

Makes enough to frost a 9 × 13-inch cake

No-Bake Chocolate Pie

Good summer or winter, this pie comes together in seconds. A word of caution:
It's very rich. Use nonfat whipped topping to cut fat and calories.

One 8-ounce container frozen
whipped topping, thawed
1/3 cup chocolate syrup

One ready-made graham cracker
crust (or see recipe on page 160)

In a medium mixing bowl, combine whipped topping and syrup until completely blended.
Pour into prepared crust and smooth over. Cover and freeze for at least three hours before serving.

Serves 6

No-Bake Yogurt Pie

In the summer, the last thing I want to do is turn on my oven. Here's a very simple pie that lets you avoid that. You need to make it ahead, since it has to freeze for 4 hours in order to set properly. Get creative and use any combination of yogurt or fruit. (I use peach yogurt with canned strawberries, peaches, or raspberries.) Also, try low- or nonfat yogurt and whipped topping to cut calories and fat.

One 15-ounce can fruit, drained

1½ cups (two 8-ounce containers) flavored yogurt

1 cup frozen whipped topping, thawed

1 ready-made 9-inch graham cracker pie crust (or see recipe on page 160)

Mash the fruit with a fork so that it's not whole (unless you're using blueberries; they're small enough). Add the yogurt and whipped topping, and stir until combined. Pour the mixture into the pie crust. Cover (I turn over the plastic insert the premade crusts come with and use that as a cover), and chill in the freezer for at least 4 hours. Bring the pie out 30 minutes before serving time and put it in the refrigerator to soften a little.

Serves 6 to 8

Maple-Walnut Pie

This is a nice winter treat suitable for holiday entertaining. Try it instead of pecan pie sometime.

One ready-made 9-inch pie crust	**3 eggs**
1/3 cup (5 tablespoons plus 1 teaspoon) **butter**	**2/3 cup brown sugar**
	Pinch salt
1 cup walnuts (whole or broken)	**1 cup pure maple syrup**

Preheat the oven to 350°F. Prepare the pie crust according to the package directions.

Melt the butter and set it aside. Line the bottom of the pie crust with walnuts. In a medium mixing bowl, combine the eggs, brown sugar, salt, and maple syrup. Stir until smooth. Add the melted butter, taking care that it's not so hot that it will curdle the eggs. Pour the maple mixture into the pie crust and set it on the next-to-lowest rack in the oven.

Bake for 50 minutes, or until the edges are browning and the middle of the pie is almost set (a knife inserted off-center should come out clean). Let the pie cool on a rack for at least 10 minutes, then chill in the refrigerator. Serve cold or at room temperature.

Serves 6 to 8

Note: The pie puffs up during baking but settles back down again as it cools.

Drinks

CHAPTER 13

Almond Milk

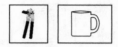

Flavoring milk was a common way to get kids to drink it when I was a kid, but the powders were loaded with sugar. Here's a way to add flavor without so much sugar. This makes an ideal beverage to go with snacks, breakfast cereals (including hot oatmeal), or dessert.

1 cup evaporated milk or whole milk (chilled)

¹/₈ to ¹/₄ teaspoon almond extract

¹/₄ to ¹/₂ teaspoon sugar or artificial sweetener to taste

Combine all of the ingredients in a mug or glass.

Serves 1

VARIATION

Hot Almond Milk

Follow the recipe above but heat it in the microwave on high in a microwave-safe mug for about 1¹/₂ minutes. You may also heat it in a saucepan over medium heat.

Hot Buttered Caramel Milk

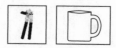

It's not as decadent as it sounds, but boy, is it good. This is a terrific holiday beverage, especially for those wishing to forego the even more calorie- and alcohol-laden eggnog.

2 tablespoons packed brown sugar	**$^1/_8$ teaspoon vanilla extract**
1 cup evaporated milk or whole milk	**$^1/_4$ to $^1/_2$ teaspoon butter**

Microwave Directions

Place the brown sugar in the bottom of a mug. Add the milk and vanilla, then microwave on high for about 1½ minutes. Stir, and float the butter on the top.

Stovetop Directions

Put the milk in a small saucepan over medium heat. Cook until hot, stirring occasionally. Put the sugar in the bottom of a mug, add the milk and vanilla, and stir. Float the butter on top.

Serves 1

Vanilla Milk

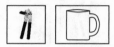

Trying to avoid chocolate or just want something different? Vanilla milk satisfies the desire for a sweeter taste quite well, without a whole lot of sugar. Use low-fat milk to cut calories.

1 cup evaporated milk or whole milk
   (chilled)

¼ to ½ teaspoon vanilla extract
   (to taste)

Sweetener to taste (about
   ½ teaspoon sugar or sugar substitute)

Combine all of the ingredients in a glass or mug. Serve chilled.

Serves 1

VARIATION

Hot Vanilla Milk

Follow the recipe above but heat it in the microwave on high in a microwave-safe mug for about 1 to 1½ minutes. You can also heat it in a saucepan over medium heat. You may need to increase the vanilla by another ¼ teaspoon. Makes a good hot breakfast or dessert beverage.

Chocolate-Almond Coffee

I find that a little sweetener brings out the flavor of this drink, although those of you who drink your coffee "straight" may opt to forgo it. (If you don't want to use sugar, try about ½ packet of pink sugar substitute or a whole packet of blue.)

1 cup brewed coffee
¼ teaspoon almond extract
¼ teaspoon vanilla extract
¼ teaspoon unsweetened cocoa
    powder

Cream and sugar or artificial
    sweetener

Add the almond and vanilla extracts and the cocoa to your brewed coffee and stir until dissolved. Add cream and sweetener if desired. (Remember that evaporated milk, including the non-fat variety, makes a great "half-and-half" creamer.)

Serves 1

Almond Tea

There's a lovely undercurrent of almond in this tea, making it a wonderful snack with fortune cookies in the afternoon, or a satisfying tea after Asian cuisine. It also makes a superb iced tea.

1 regular tea bag
¹/₄ teaspoon vanilla extract
¹/₈ teaspoon almond extract

1 teaspoon sugar or 1 packet sugar
    substitute

Heat 1 cup of water and make tea as directed on the package. Stir in the vanilla and almond extracts and sweetener of choice. Serve hot.

Serves 1

Apricot Nectar

According to the label, a ½-cup serving of canned apricots will supply about 20 percent of your daily vitamin A requirement. And it's all natural.

One 15-ounce can apricot halves   **1 teaspoon sugar** (optional)

Puree the apricots with their juice. Add the sugar if desired. (Taste first, especially if you used apricots in heavy syrup.)

Makes 1½ cups

Apricot-Orange Freeze

We used to make something like this as kids, only we used raw eggs in it. Luckily, what we didn't know didn't hurt us.

One 15-ounce can apricot halves	**2 teaspoons vanilla extract**
One 12-ounce can or bottle orange juice (1½ cups)	**1 tablespoon sugar** (optional)
	2 cups crushed ice

Puree the apricots with their juice. Stir in the orange juice, vanilla, and sugar, if desired. Add the crushed ice and puree until blended.

Makes 4 cups

Sour-Cherry Freeze

Check your label to be sure, but tart pie cherries have only about 175 calories per can. That breaks down to about 50 per drink, plus whatever sugar you add. If you don't want to add sugar, try your favorite substitute and you've got a lower-calorie fruit drink. Makes a great "slush" for the kids or a good base for a daiquiri-type rum drink.

One 15-ounce can tart pie cherries   **2 cups crushed ice**
3 tablespoons sugar

Pour the cherries (with their juice) into a blender and puree. Add the sugar and crushed ice and puree until smooth.

Makes about 3 1/2 cups

Cranberry Yogurt Whip

This is a recipe I developed by adapting a recipe for mango *lassi,* a traditional Indian beverage. I find cranberry sauce to be very sweet, so I have listed sugar as an optional ingredient. If it's for kids, they'll probably want sugar. You could also add vanilla ice cream to make a milk shake. Keep this drink in mind during the holidays—you can use nonfat yogurt to cut calories.

One 16-ounce can whole-berry cranberry sauce
3 cups plain yogurt
(net wt. 32 ounces)

¼ cup sugar (optional)
2 cups crushed ice (see Note)

Process the cranberry sauce in the blender until it's no longer jellied. Add the remaining ingredients and process until smooth.

Serves 6

Note: If you don't have a refrigerator with a crushed-ice function, first process ice cubes with your blender until you get 2 cups' worth.

Fruit Soda

For best results, all juices and sodas should be chilled first. If they're not cold, you may pour them over crushed ice, but this will dilute the flavor a little. Use diet soda to cut calories if you wish.

Two 12-ounce cans lemon-lime soda
  (3 cups)
2 cups cranberry juice

1 cup pineapple juice
1/2 cup orange juice
2 teaspoons bottled lime juice

Combine all of the ingredients in a pitcher. Serve chilled.

Makes about 6 1/2 cups

Easy Orange Essence Tea

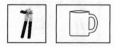

I like to have choices, which is why I like to keep basic things on hand and flavor them as I wish. Orange-spice tea can be far more expensive than regular tea. With this method, you can make it easily whenever you like. You can find orange extract where you find vanilla and spices in your grocery store.

1 regular tea bag	**Sweetener** (optional)
¼ to ½ teaspoon orange extract	**1 cinnamon stick** (optional)

Heat 1 cup of water and brew the tea according to the package directions. Stir in the orange extract. Add sweetener and a cinnamon stick if desired.

Note: You may add orange extract to tea that has already been iced; however, the cinnamon stick works best if used in hot tea first. (By the way, I usually find cinnamon sticks to be less expensive in my grocer's Mexican foods spices section.)

Pear Nectar

Serve this drink chilled. You can chill it in advance by simply keeping a can of pears in the refrigerator. If you serve it over ice, you may need to add a little extra lemon juice and sugar to taste, as the water dilutes the flavor.

One 15-ounce can pears (in light or heavy syrup)

1 teaspoon bottled lemon juice

Puree the pears with their syrup and lemon juice until smooth. Chill and serve.

Serves 2

Pineapple Fizz

You may use pineapples in heavy syrup or the no-sugar-added type for this. If you use the no-sugar-added variety, you may want to add a little sugar. (Try a couple of tablespoonfuls at a time.) Also, feel free to use diet lemon-lime soda.

One 15-ounce can crushed pineapple **2 cups lemon-lime soda** (diet soda is
1 teaspoon bottled lemon juice   okay)
2 cups crushed ice (see Note)   **Sugar to taste** (optional)

Process the pineapple, juice and all, and lemon juice in the blender until pureed. Add the ice and process until smooth. Gently stir in the soda. Add sugar if desired.

Note: If you don't have a refrigerator with a crushed ice dispenser, first process ice cubes in your blender until you have 2 cups' worth.

Makes 5 cups

Pineapple Ice

Feel free to use no-sugar-added pineapple or pineapple in heavy syrup. If you use the no-sugar-added variety, you may want to add a little sugar. (Try a couple of tablespoonfuls at a time.)

One 15-ounce can crushed pineapple   **Sugar to taste** (optional)
2 cups crushed ice (see Note)

Process the pineapples, juice and all, in the blender until pureed. Add the ice and process until smooth. Add sugar if desired.

Note: If you don't have a refrigerator with a crushed ice dispenser, first process ice cubes in your blender until you have 2 cups' worth.

Makes 3 cups

"Sham"pagne

Perfect as a party drink, mock champagne is also nice around the holidays for those not wishing to imbibe too much alcohol. You can use diet ginger ale to cut calories without cutting flavor. Make sure everything is chilled before you start. If your ingredients are not chilled, you can pour them over crushed ice; it just won't look like the real thing. (For a festive look, add a maraschino cherry to each glass.) This recipe can easily be doubled or tripled for large groups.

2 cups soda water

2 cups ginger ale

1 1/2 cups unsweetened white grape juice or apple juice

The ingredients should all be chilled. Combine them in a pitcher and serve in champagne glasses.

Makes 5 1/2 cups (fills 11 champagne flutes three-quarters full)

Vanilla Cola

This is so easy and it's great when you want to have a variety of sodas on hand for kids and guests. Plus, you can use your favorite cola brand (mine's whatever's on sale), including a diet version. What's more, it makes a great float if you add ice cream.

1 cup cola   **1 teaspoon vanilla extract**

Add the vanilla to the cola and stir gently. Serve over ice.

Serves 1

Menu Suggestions

APPENDIX 1

BREAKFAST OR BRUNCH

Baked Egg Squares with Pesto, Cheese, and Artichoke
Sourdough toast
"Sham"pagne

Southwestern Egg Bake
Cornbread
Easy Orange Essence Tea

Creamy Three-Cheese Quiche
Grandma's Biscuits
Chocolate-Almond Coffee

Ham and Cheese Scramble
Molasses Wheat Bread
Pineapple Fizz

Cinnamon-Apple Pancakes
Caramel Syrup
Almond Tea

LUNCH OR DINNER

Faux Guacamole with Corn Chips
Black Bean and Corn Chowder
Baked Cornbread Chiles Rellenos
Corn and Kidney Bean Salad
Sweet Potato Cake

Cajun Cheese Dip with Crackers or Vegetables
Barbecued Chicken Pizza
Quick Potato Salad
Southern Succotash
Old-Fashioned Cherry Cobbler

Indian-Spiced Snack Mix
Grandma's Vegetable Soup
Chicken and Potato Curry
Green Beans Amandine
Sour Cream–Banana Cake with Milk Chocolate Frosting

Corn and Tomato Salad
Beef Shepherd's Pie
Cheesy Hominy and Sour Cream
Cranberry Sorbet

Sun-Dried Tomato and Cheese Spread with Crackers or Vegetables
Corn, Red Pepper, and Cheese Salad
Gazpacho
Southwestern Turkey Stew
Apple-Raisin Bread Pudding

Curried Shrimp Dip
Spicy Noodle, Cashew, and Chicken Stir-Fry
Pineapple-Orange Salad
Dilled Green Beans
Coconut Cake with Brown Sugar Frosting

Corn, Red Pepper, and Cheese Salad
Mexican Chicken Bake
Tex-Mex Spiced Black Beans
Cheesy Spanish Rice
Caramel Cream Pie

Italian-Herbed Artichoke Squares
Spinach Soup
Falafel with Minted Yogurt Sauce
Chickpea, Tomato, and Olive Salad with Lemon Basil Vinaigrette
No-Bake Yogurt Pie

Cream of Artichoke Soup
Chicken Pastitsio
Green Bean and Beet Salad
Tomatoes with Basil and Oregano
Coconut Custard

Mediterranean White Bean Dip with Baguettes, Crackers, or Vegetables
Penne with Spicy Tomato-Cheese Sauce
Dilled Green Beans
Parmesan Rolls
French Apple Cheesecake

Pesto-Cheese Spread with Baguettes, Crackers, or Vegetables
Chicken Caesar Salad
Baked Ziti
Sautéed Artichokes
Caramel Pecan Pie

Tarragon Tuna Dip with Crackers or Vegetables
Salmon Chowder
Pasta with Lemon, Basil, and Clams
Greek Green Beans
Chocolate-Raspberry Pie

Red Pepper Jam with Crackers or Toasted Cockail Rye Bread
Crab Tostadas with Cumin-Lime-Mint Dressing
Salmon Croquettes with Lemon Horseradish Sauce
New Potatoes in Sour Cream and Dill
Cranberry Sorbet

No-Cook Peach Soup
Salmon-Orange Salad with Ginger-Lime Dressing
Seafood Lasagna
Dilled Green Beans
Easy Coconut Macaroons

Stocking Your Pantry

APPENDIX 2

One of the advantages to using this cookbook is that most of the ingredients you need keep very well, which cuts down on trips to the store. You can reduce those trips even further by keeping certain staples on hand. You may even want to photocopy this list as a general shopping guide, starting with your known favorites and then building your stores over time.

Standard Canned Items
  Chicken
  Chicken broth
  Condensed cream of mushroom, chicken, celery soup
  Corn—whole-kernel and cream-style
  Evaporated milk (12-ounce cans)
  Green beans
  Onions
  Peaches
  Pears
  Potatoes, sliced and small round
  Roast beef
  Salmon
  Sliced mushrooms
  Sliced black olives
  Sweet young peas

Tomatoes—crushed, diced, paste, puree, sauce
Tuna
Turkey

For Special Occasions or Occasional Use

Artichoke bottoms/hearts
Asparagus (white or green)
Baby-food bananas, carrots, plums, butternut squash
Beans—black, pinto, small white, cannellini
Beets
Capers
Carrots
Chilies, diced green and jalapeño
Crab
Garbanzo beans
Kidney beans
Mandarin oranges
Pesto sauce
Plums
Raspberries
Roasted red peppers
Shrimp
Spinach
Sun-dried tomatoes
Sweetened condensed milk

Flavorings

Cocoa powder
Horseradish
Lemon juice (bottled)
Lime juice (bottled)
Oils (olive, safflower, peanut, soybean)

Soy sauce
Vinegar
Wine (red, white, cream sherry)
Worcestershire sauce

Other Items
Almonds
Baking powder
Baking soda
Butter
Cheese—Cheddar, Jack, Swiss, real grated Parmesan (not the powdered kind)
Corn syrup
Cornstarch
Eggs
Flour—all-purpose
Frozen pie crusts or pastry dough
Maple syrup
Mayonnaise
Pasta (spaghetti, fettuccine, linguine, penne)
Peanut butter
Pine nuts
Raisins or currants
Rice
Sugar
Walnuts
Whipped Topping

Spices
Allspice
Basil
Bay leaf
Cayenne

Celery salt

Chili powder

Cilantro flakes or ground coriander

Cinnamon (ground)

Cloves (ground)

Cumin (ground)

Curry powder

Dill

Garlic powder (*not* garlic salt)

Ginger (ground)

Marjoram

Mint leaves (dried)

Mustard powder

Nutmeg (ground)

Onion powder (*not* onion salt)

Oregano

Paprika

Parsley

Pepper

Rosemary

Sage

Salt

Tarragon

Thyme

Although the above is a suggested guide, you may really like something I didn't mention or you may detest something I did. Canned spinach, for instance. I'm probably not the only one for whom it conjures memories of school hot lunches with the wet, seaweedlike mass nestled between the burned fish sticks and the hot molten apple compote. And let's not forget the smell. . . . But put that spinach into a soup and I'll happily eat it. Heck, I don't even remember where it came from. Which is sort of the point of all this. That, and you should eat the food you like, and make your food the way you like it.

Food and Flavoring Substitutions

1 tablespoon cornstarch	=	2 tablespoons all-purpose flour (for thickening purposes)
1 teaspoon baking powder	=	½ teaspoon cream of tartar plus ¼ teaspoon baking soda and ¼ teaspoon cornstarch
1 cup buttermilk	=	1 tablespoon lemon juice or vinegar plus enough milk to make 1 cup (let stand for 5 minutes before using)
1 tablespoon onion powder or ¼ cup instant chopped onion	=	1 medium-sized onion, chopped (about ⅔ cup)
⅛ teaspoon garlic powder	=	1 clove garlic
1 teaspoon dry leafy herbs	=	1 tablespoon fresh leafy herbs
½ teaspoon dehydrated lemon or orange peel	=	1 teaspoon grated orange or lemon peel
¾ cup cracker crumbs	=	1 cup bread crumbs

Measurements and Equivalents

APPENDIX 4

3 teaspoons	=	1 tablespoon				
2 tablespoons	=	1 ounce	=	1/8 cup		
4 tablespoons	=	2 ounces	=	1/4 cup		
5 1/3 tablespoons	=	3 ounces	=	1/3 cup		
8 tablespoons	=	4 ounces	=	1/2 cup		
10 2/3 tablespoons	=	5 ounces	=	2/3 cup		
12 tablespoons	=	6 ounces	=	3/4 cup		
16 tablespoons	=	8 ounces	=	1 cup		
16 ounces	=	2 cups	=	1 pint		
32 ounces	=	4 cups	=	2 pints	=	1 quart
128 ounces	=	16 cups	=	4 quarts	=	1 gallon
16 ounces	=	1 pound				

⫙ PANS AND DISHES

4-cup dish	=	9-inch pie plate, 8-inch cake pan, or 7 × 3-inch loaf pan
6-cup dish	=	9-inch cake pan, 10-inch pie plate, or 8 × 4-inch loaf pan
8-cup or 2-quart dish	=	8 × 8-inch square pan, 11 × 7-inch baking pan, or 9 × 5-inch loaf pan
10-cup dish	=	9 × 9-inch square pan or 15 × 10-inch jelly roll pan
12-cup or 3-quart dish	=	13 × 9 × 2-inch baking pan
16-cup dish or 4-quart dish	=	13 × 9 × 3-inch roasting pan

Index